C000178350

hamlyn

MARTINI

David Taylor

Notes

The measure that has been used in the recipes is based on a bar measure, which is 25 ml (1 fl oz). If preferred, a different volume can be used providing the proportions are kept constant within a drink and suitable adjustments are made to spoon measurements, where they occur.

Standard level spoon measurements are used in all recipes.
1 tablespoon = one 15 ml spoon
1 teaspoon = one 5 ml spoon
Imperial and metric measurements have been given in some of the recipes. Use one set of measurements only.

US	UK
granulated sugar	caster sugar
maraschino cherries	cocktail cherries
toothpick	cocktail stick
heavy cream	double cream
presweetened cocoa powder	drinking chocolate
confectioners' sugar	icing sugar
pitcher	jug
lemon peel or zest	lemon rind
light cream	single cream
club soda	soda water

SAFETY NOTE The American Egg Board advises that eggs should not be consumed raw. This book contains recipes made with raw eggs. It is prudent for more vulnerable people such as pregnant and nursing mothers, invalids, the elderly, babies and young children to avoid these recipes.

First published in Great Britain in 2002 by
Hamlyn, a division of Octopus Publishing Group Ltd
2–4 Heron Quays, London E14 4JP

Copyright © Octopus Publishing Group Ltd 2002

ISBN 0 600 60712 7

A CIP catalogue record for this book is available from the British Library

Printed and bound in China

10 9 8 7 6 5 4 3 2 1

Contents

INTRODUCTION   4

FROM THE BEGINNING   6

MARTINI MIXOLOGY   38

MARTINIS IN THE MOVIES   50

IN THE LOUNGE   76

GLOSSARY   94

INDEX AND ACKNOWLEDGMENTS   96

Introduction

'When I have one Martini, I feel bigger, wiser, taller.
When I have the second, I feel superlative.
When I have more, there's no holding me.'

William Faulkner

The perfect Martini is crystal clear to the eye, chilled to the lips, dry to the tongue.

Few drinks have come to signify so much to so many. Yet its sophistication lies in its sheer simplicity. Certain select ingredients, mixed to perfection and served with just a subtle hint of garnish. In short, class in a glass.

How strange, then, to consider that the Martini started life as yellowish-hued, insufferably sweet hotchpotch of liquors thrown together almost on a whim. Or that its rise to fame came at a time when America was undergoing one of its most notoriously lawless eras. Or that it was once dismissed as a museum-piece left over from the class war and – even worse – an irrelevance.

But the Martini prevailed.

From the Beginning...

In the beginning, there was gin – or, more accurately, there was genever. In 1650, Dr Franciscus de la Boie, the medical professor at the University of Leyden in Holland, came up with the idea of mixing the oil of juniper berries with grain alcohol as a treatment for kidney disorders. He called it genever, after the French word for juniper.

The Dutch had been distilling a type of liqueur from juniper berries for centuries. In the late 1500s, British troops fighting against the Spanish in the Netherlands during the Dutch War of Independence eagerly lapped up this potent local beverage, nicknaming it 'Dutch Courage'. They also spread the word of their discovery back home. Where Dr de la Boie's genius lay was in mixing the juniper extract with grain alcohol, making it closer to whiskey than to brandy.

FROM GENEVER TO GIN

Genever was quick and cheap to produce and, thanks to its pleasant taste, proved popular with patients. It was inevitable that it would eventually gain a foothold in the rest of Europe. Scarcely a decade later, in 1660, the great London diarist Samuel Pepys recorded that he had cured a case of colic by using a mixture of 'strong water made with juniper'.

When William of Orange and his wife Mary drove James II from the throne of England in 1689, the Dutch Protestant monarch attempted to stifle imports of brandies from Catholic countries by imposing higher duties and deregulating the local production of grain alcohol. Thus the distilling of gin proliferated in England and, without too much prompting, spread around the world.

THE ADVENT OF VERMOUTH

Vermouth was devised as a treatment for intestinal worms. The name was derived from *wermut*, the German word for the plant wormwood. An extract from the flowers was blended with brandy, light wine, herbs, spices and barks to give vermouth its distinctive taste.

Although there have been mentions of a similar aromatized wine as far back in time as both the Greek and Roman empires, what we would recognize as vermouth was only established as a drink in the late 1700s and enjoyed a surge in popularity in the 19th century.

France and Italy became the world's leading producers of vermouth. The Italians favoured a sweet red variety. By far the most famous name in Italian vermouth production was the Distilleria Nazionale da Spirito di Vino, based in Torino, which changed its name to Martini & Rossi in 1879. The French, however, preferred a dry white variety, which was first produced by the company Noilly Prat at the south-coast port of Marseillan in 1813.

COMING TOGETHER

Who originally had the brainwave of mixing gin and vermouth together, thus creating the first Martini? This is a matter of some controversy, as we will see.

THE 'PROFESSOR' AND THE MINER

Some people think the first Martini was mixed by 'Professor' Jerry Thomas, the bartender of the Occidental Hotel in San Francisco, sometime during the early 1860s when the frontier outpost was experiencing a boom. In 1859, the 'Comstock Lode' – a seam of gold and silver over 30m (100ft) wide and over 3km (2 miles) long – had been discovered in the Great Basin Mountains and anyone who had ever swung a pickaxe came to the West Coast to stake their claim.

The story goes that an itinerant miner, bound for the East Bay town of Martinez some 65km (40 miles) away, wandered into the Occidental and asked the 'Prof' to mix him up something special.

The miner must have been suitably impressed, because Thomas later included a recipe for the drink – under the name Gin Cocktail – in his *Bon-Vivant's Companion, or How To Mix Drinks*, first published in 1862. Later, in the 1887 edition of the book, he changed the name to the Martinez Cocktail, in honour of its first ever fan.

The Occidental Hotel on Montgomery Road, San Francisco.

MARTINEZ OR MARTINI?

There can be no doubt that the cocktail served up by Thomas eventually did become known as the Martinez and did resemble the modern-day Martini, but someone else had already used that name. In 1884, three years before Thomas renamed his Gin Cocktail the Martinez, O.H. Byron's book *The Modern Bartender* had included a similar recipe under that title.

Harry Johnson also published a version of the drink in his 1888 book *The New and Improved Illustrated Bartender's Manual, or How To Mix Drinks of the Present Style*, calling it the Martine.

To complicate matters, the citizens of the town of Martinez insisted that the cocktail had actually been first mixed by their local bartender, Julio Richelieu. In their version of events, the legendary miner arrived in town and wandered into Richelieu's saloon, offering a gold nugget in exchange for a bottle of whiskey. Feeling that he had been short-changed by the deal, the miner got Richelieu to mix him up a supplementary drink, and the Martinez was born. The residents of Martinez even erected a brass plaque in their town to commemorate the birth of the cocktail.

THE EAST COAST VERSION

The Martinez and the modern Martini are similar but not identical. Jerry Thomas's Martinez was predominantly vermouth, with the gin thrown in almost as an afterthought. It also had a shot of Old Tom gin, a British variety far sweeter than the ultra-dry London gin. The sweetness was enhanced by two dashes of Maraschino and a dash of orange bitters. The mixed drink would have had a yellow hue, due to impurities.

A New York City bartender, called Martini di Arma di Taggia, claimed it was he who had mixed the first real Dry Martini in 1912.

> '... the supreme
> American gift to
> world culture.'
>
> *American author Bernard de Voto*
>
> *describing the Martini*

Led astray: Shelley Winters rekindles old flame William Powell over a Martini in Take One False Step (1949).

Dry Martini

ice cubes
½ measure dry vermouth
4 drops orange bitters
2½ measures gin
1 green olive or lemon twist

This is the traditional Dry Martini, flavoured with orange bitters and dry vermouth.

Fill the mixing glass with ice cubes and add the vermouth and orange bitters. Stir until the ice cubes are thoroughly coated then pour off the excess. Pour in the gin and stir thoroughly then strain the cocktail into a chilled glass. Drop an olive or a lemon twist into the mixed drink and serve.

'Happiness is finding two olives in your Martini when you're hungry.'

American talk-show host Johnny Carson

Paula Prentiss covets Rock Hudson's Martini in Man's Favourite Sport (1964).

Classic Dry Martini

Sometimes called the naked Martini, this cocktail is far drier then the original Dry Martini.

½ measure dry vermouth
3 measures frozen gin
1 green olive or lemon twist

Swirl the vermouth round the inside of a chilled Martini glass then discard the excess. Pour in the frozen gin, add an olive or lemon twist and serve.

VARIATIONS There are several variations to this classic cocktail. The Dickens is a straightforward drink served without any kind of embellishment. The Gibson is decorated with 2 cocktail onions and the Franklin with 2 green olives, while the Bradford is prepared in a cocktail shaker and shaken rather than stirred.

He named it after himself and served it up to the millionaire and philanthropist John D. Rockefeller at the Knickerbocker Hotel. Di Taggia's recipe called for equal measures of London gin and dry white vermouth with a dash of orange bitters, which was certainly closer to the modern Martini than the Martinez. Rockefeller was teetotal, however, and unlikely to have ordered the drink.

Di Taggia's recipe was not revolutionary either. In 1896, Thomas Stuart published *Stuart's Fancy Drinks and How to Make Them*, in which his recipe for a gin-based cocktail – called a Marguerite – stipulated one measure of dry gin to a half measure of dry vermouth, with a dash of bitters. Di Taggia can't even lay claim to the name. In Jack London's 1910 novel *Burning Daylight*, the hero quaffs Martinis at all hours. The truth is that, by the time di Taggia surfaced, variations of the Martini were in bars and recipe books all over the States.

WHAT'S IN A NAME?

If di Taggia didn't come up with the name Martini, who did? Some have suggested that the drink was named after the Martini Henry rifle – a Swiss firearm invented by Friedreich von Martini and used by the British Army between 1871 and 1890 – on account of its formidable 'kick'. This is obviously untrue, as the drink predated the gun. The *Oxford English Dictionary*, traditionally the last word on most subjects, is of no use here. It attributes the cocktail to the respected Italian vermouth maker Martini & Rossi. However, the company specialized in sweet red vermouth – never an ingredient of the Dry Martini – and didn't even begin exporting to the Americas until 1867. By that time, the French company Noilly Prat had been trading their dry vermouth with the States for over a decade.

So, attempting to establish the true origin of the Martini and its name is almost impossible.

GOING GLOBAL

As the world entered what author F. Scott Fitzgerald was to dub 'The Jazz Age', Martinis were being shaken all over America, and no one really cared who had invented them. Their fame was growing, too. As news spread of the new-fangled American fad for cocktails, the rest of the world decided they wanted to join the party. Martinis became the rage in all the major capitals of Europe – there has even been a suggestion that it was in London that the humble olive became the garnish of choice.

Yet, even as the Martini began to thrive all around the world, a seismic shift in the political scene in America meant that the drink might have to disappear completely. This movement was summed up neatly in one word: Prohibition.

DRYING OUT – PROHIBITION

There had been a temperance movement in America almost from the moment that the Pilgrim Fathers arrived, but it was only with the

LONDON DRY

Few authors caught the spirit of the age quite like Jack London. In Burning Daylight *(1910), Elam Harnish, a gold prospector, draws odd looks from genteel society by ordering a Martini after midnight: '... he had long since learned that Martinis had their strictly appointed times and places. But he liked Martinis and, being a natural man, he chose deliberately to drink when and how he pleased.'*

creation of the Anti-Saloon League in 1893 that the movement gained real political teeth. The League was concerned not only with the antisocial effects of drinking but also with the very existence of drinking places. They began to lobby the government aggressively to have such establishments outlawed.

In a sense, saloons had become victims of their own success. By the turn of the 20th century, the brewers and distillers of America numbered among the most profitable companies in the country. As a result, bars and saloons had proliferated. Faced with this increase in competition, saloon owners had brought gambling and prostitution onto their premises to draw custom from their rivals. Confronted with the facts, it was hard to argue with the Anti-Saloon League's argument that such venues had become dens of vice and corruption.

World War One gave the League even more ammunition. The League members said that brewers were damaging the war effort by debilitating the military and the national workforce. They also thought that the influx of immigrants from Europe in the years leading up to the war had produced a detrimental effect on the character of the nation. The immigrants, they argued, were corrupting the country through their lax attitude towards alcohol, and were also responsible for an increase in crime. It was hard to address any of the League's arguments without being branded anti-American.

Against the Law As more and more politicians were won over to the League's cause, so Prohibition became inevitable. Thus the 18th Amendment, which outlawed the manufacture, sale,

Girl Power: The women's temperance movement of Madison, Minnesota campaign for the prohibition of alcohol in 1917.

transportation or import of alcoholic beverages, was added to the US Constitution in 1918. In the following year, the Volstead Act, which gave effect to that Amendment, was enacted by the US Congress. It came into effect at midnight on 16 January 1920. America had become a teetotal nation. Or had it?

GOING UNDERGROUND

Even before the 18th Amendment came into effect, there was trouble. Thieves broke into a government warehouse used to hold impounded liquor, and walked off with half a million dollars' worth of booze. And this was just the start.

Rough liquor: a makeshift speakeasy bar.

When the Prohibition laws were first mooted, grand plans were made to finance a re-education scheme to teach the public the virtues of teetotalism. Agents of the law were also assured that they would be given the resources necessary to police the situation. But the money to put these plans into effect failed to materialize.

The country's bars and saloons may have been closed down, but in their place had sprung up a thriving black market, so vast that the various law-enforcement agencies had neither the funds nor the manpower to stop it. America was overrun by smugglers and bootleggers. There were 62,747 arrests for liquor violations in 1925 alone, and 172,537 illicit breweries and distilleries seized in the same years. Even doctors joined in, supplementing their income by writing bogus prescriptions for whiskey for medicinal purposes. The demand for sacramental wine used in church services increased by 800,000 gallons between 1922 and 1924.

Bribery and Corruption In 1926, New York politician Fiorella H. LaGuardia, an active opponent of Prohibition, reported to the US Senate: 'In my opinion, such an enormous traffic in liquor could not be carried out without the knowledge, if not the connivance, of the officials entrusted with the enforcement of the law ... It is my calculation that at least $1 million a day is paid in graft and corruption to Federal State and local officers ... I will concede that that the saloon was odious, but now we have delicatessen stores, pool rooms, drug stores, millinery shops, private parlors and 57 other varieties of speakeasies selling liquor and flourishing ...'

The term 'speakeasy' had originally been coined to cover just about any establishment that sold booze 'under the counter', but it gradually became synonymous with a very particular type of secret drinking club.

`... with a bang of bad booze, flappers with bare legs, jangled morals and wild weekends'

– Hoagy Carmichael, on how the 1920s came in

*Getting in a flap: the world of the 1920s speakeasy was exposed in the movie **Queen of the Night Clubs** (1929), a highly fictionalized biography of New York hostess 'Texas' Guinan in which she played herself.*

SPEAKEASIES AND THE MOB

The speakeasies – secret drinking clubs for which you needed a password to gain entry – were the real precursors of the modern cocktail lounge, offering their customers a comfortable refuge from the Prohibition laws, often serving booze in coffee cups to disguise the contents. The most famous jazz and blues musicians of the time – such as Duke Ellington, Fats Waller, Bix Beiderbecke and Bessie Smith – were booked to provide entertainment.

In the speakeasies, bartenders often experimented with drinks, inventing such future 'standards' as Long Island Iced Tea (the name was a code intended to subvert Prohibition laws) and the Highball. Like the saloons before them, the speakeasies frequently doubled

THE TEXAS ROSE

Anyone who frequented New York speakeasies in the 1920s and 1930s knew 'Texas' Guinan (pictured below). She was born Mary Guinan in Waco, Texas, but changed her name when she went to Hollywood and played a cowgirl in silent Westerns. She moved to New York and accepted a job running the King Cole Room at the Knickerbocker Hotel. When gangster Larry Fay opened a speakeasy on West 54th Street, 'Texas' agreed to front the operation. Every time their club was busted, Guinan and Fay reopened somewhere else under a different name. Her customers always knew where to find her.

as gambling dens and brothels. It was estimated that there were anywhere between 200,000 and 500,000 such establishments operating throughout the USA during the Prohibition years.

Most of the speakeasies were either owned by the Mob, as the Mafia was popularly called, or were only able to operate due to their Mob connections. The mobsters operated their own bootlegging operations or facilitated the passage of smuggled liquor from Canada and Europe. They also ran protection rackets to keep rivals at bay. As the crime syndicates became ever more organized, the mobsters became as popular as celebrities, exuding a dangerous glamour that caught the imagination of the public.

For the most part, the authorities were either helpless to stem the tide of illicit drink – FBI agent Eliot Ness and his Untouchables may have been depicted as fearless crimebusters in popular folklore, but they actually achieved very little in stopping the likes of Chicago Mob boss Al Capone from flourishing – or else took generous bribes to turn a blind eye to their operation.

As the speakeasies flourished, so did the Martini.

BOOTLEG GIN

Up until the 1920s, whiskey had been the alcoholic spirit of choice in America. But then gin – by that time the main ingredient of the Martini – overtook it. There was a very good reason for this – whiskey simply took too long to produce. The production of a decent whiskey relied on a lengthy ageing process for which the bootleggers had no patience. So instead they turned to gin.

Because it required no ageing, a quality gin could be distilled both faster and cheaper than any whiskey. All you needed was a large container into which to pour the ingredients – even a bathtub would do, prompting the rise in 'bathtub gin'. Such improvised 'gin mills' sprang up in sheds and back rooms all around the country, ensuring a ready supply for all.

THE END IN SIGHT

By the end of the 1920s, the writing was on the wall. With the stock-market crash of 1929 heralding the beginning of the Great Depression, it must have been obvious that the attempts to destroy what had once been one of the most profitable industries in America had been spectacularly ill-timed.

Many politicians were already of the opinion that Prohibition had been a disaster. Pressure groups had sprung up to lobby for a repeal of the Volstead Act, most notably the Association Against the Prohibition Amendment (which, ironically, was partly funded by the teetotal John D. Rockefeller, who had by now abandoned his former support of the Anti-Saloon League). All it needed was a President with the nerve to alienate voters in favour of Prohibition and perform a complete U-turn on government policy. Franklin Delano Roosevelt was the man for the job.

A woman models a 'rummy apron' for the smuggling of booze.

The long arm of the law: police officers in Washingon DC display an impounded consignment of moonshine.

Gimlet

2 measures gin
1 measure lime cordial
ice cubes
water, to taste (½ measure
  is about right)
lime wedge

This is a slightly sweet Martini with a pronounced citrus flavour from the lime cordial.

Put the gin and lime cordial into a mixing glass, fill up with ice cubes and stir well. Strain into a chilled cocktail glass and add water to taste, then squeeze the lime wedge into the cocktail before adding it to the drink.

'One is all right, two is too many and three is not enough.'

James Thurber describing the Martini

White Lady

ice cubes
1½ measures gin
¾ measure Cointreau
1 measure fresh lemon juice
¼ measure sugar syrup
(see page 95)
1 egg white
1 star fruit, to decorate

This well-known and very pleasant cocktail is a simple but quite sour-tasting drink. Star fruit is not a classic cocktail decoration but it looks highly distinctive.

Put the ice cubes into a cocktail shaker, add the gin, Cointreau, lemon juice, sugar syrup and egg white and shake well. Strain into a chilled cocktail glass and decorate with thin slices of star fruit.

THE ROUND TABLERS
– OR THE VICIOUS CIRCLE?

The Round Tablers at the Algonquin Hotel in Manhattan had an opinion about everything, including Martinis. The group had first come together at a lunch in honour of drama critic Alexander Woolcott in 1919. They were among the wittiest and most brilliant writers of their generation – Robert Benchley and Dorothy Parker of *Vanity Fair* magazine, the founder of *The New Yorker* magazine Harold Ross, playwright Marc Connelly, journalist George Kaufman, satirist James Thurber, comedian Harpo Marx and novelist Edna Ferber. The lunch was such a success that it soon became a daily event, with the group seated at one of the large, circular tables in the restaurant, filling the air with their bitchy, hilarious chatter.

A newspaper cartoonist at the time depicted the group as modern-day knights, and dubbed them the Round Tablers. However, their own private name for themselves was the Vicious Circle. Their conversations were gleefully reported in the news and tourists were soon dropping by simply to gawk at the group as they dined. On occasion, their ranks were swelled by celebrity guests, including the celebrated British writer Noël Coward and the notoriously outspoken actress Tallulah Bankhead.

The famous quote 'I must get out of these wet clothes and into a Dry Martini' has been attributed to both Robert Benchley, who supposedly said it after a day spent immersed in the water tank on the set of the movie *China Seas* in 1935, and to Alexander Woolcott, who is said to have made the remark at a party.

Dorothy Parker and her Vicious Circle.

LITERARY LIQUID

The Martini has inspired numerous writers to sing its praises. E.B. White, a lifelong contributor to *The New Yorker* magazine and author of *Stuart Little* (1945) and *Charlotte's Web* (1952), considered it to be 'the elixir of quietude' and admitted that he drank them 'the way other people take aspirin'. Herman Wouk, author of *The Caine Mutiny* (1951) and *The Winds of War* (1971), said the Martini 'sort of tastes like it isn't there at all, just a cold cloud'.

The noted American food writer M.F.K. Fisher admitted 'a well-made Martini or Gibson, correctly chilled and nicely served, has been more often my true friend than any two-legged creature'. While he was writing the classic *In Cold Blood* (1966), Truman Capote would apparently have a double Martini before lunch, another during and a 'stinger' afterwards. Editor Peter Schwed described P.G. Wodehouse's work ethic thus: 'He wrote till noon every day, then he'd watch his favourite soap and have an ice-cold Martini.'

In Kurt Vonnegut Jr's 1973 novel *Breakfast of Champions*, the title refers to the Martinis served by the waitress in the cocktail lounge of the Holiday Inn, Midland City. Vonnegut describes the novel's disillusioned hero, car salesman Dwayne Hoover, in these terms: 'Dwayne was so open to new suggestions about the meaning of life that he was easily hypnotized. So, when he looked down into his Martini, he was put into a trance by dancing myriads of winking eyes on the surface of his drink. The eyes were beads of lemon oil.'

The most evocative description is by Barnaby Conrad III, author of *The Martini: An Illustrated History of an American Classic* (1955): 'The Martini is a cocktail distilled from the wink of a platinum blonde, the sweat of a polo horse, the blast of an ocean liner's horn, the Chrysler building at sunset, a lost Cole Porter tune and the aftershave of quipping detectives in natty double breasted suits.'

DEATH BY MARTINI

In 1941, the American novelist Sherwood Anderson (pictured below), whose works included Winesburg, Ohio *(1919) and* Dark Laughter *(1925), became the first – and possibly only – person whose death could be directly attributed to a Martini. While sipping his cocktail, Anderson accidentally swallowed the cocktail stick on which his olive had been impaled. As a result of this unfortunate incident, he subsequently developed peritonitis and died.*

Aviation

ice cubes
2½ measures gin
1½ measures fresh lemon juice
½ measure Maraschino (sour cherry liqueur)
¼ measure sugar syrup (see page 95)
lemon twist

A sweet and sour Martini with a lingering flavour and a pleasant tang from the Maraschino, a liqueur made from sour cherries.

Put the ice cubes into a cocktail shaker, add the gin, lemon juice, Maraschino and sugar syrup and shake well. Strain into a chilled glass and add a lemon twist.

Dorothy Parker and her husband, Alan Campbell.

'I like to have a Martini,
But only two at the most.
After three I'm under the table,
After four I'm under the host.'

Dorothy Parker, going one better than James Thurber

Flying high: Former US President Franklin D. Roosevelt celebrates his birthday aboard a Boeing 314 flying boat in 1943.

GOODBYE TO PROHIBITION

At the Democratic Party Convention in 1932, Franklin D. Roosevelt sowed the seeds of change for America. He accepted his nomination as their presidential candidate with an impassioned speech which left little doubt as to his feelings on the subject of Prohibition: 'I congratulate this Convention for having had the courage fearlessly to write into its declaration of principles what an overwhelming majority here assembled really thinks about the 18th Amendment. This Convention wants repeal. Your candidate wants repeal. And I am confident that the United States of America wants repeal.' Roosevelt won the election and, by the end of the following year, the Volstead Act had been overturned.

MARTINIS IN THE WHITE HOUSE

Can it be pure coincidence that Roosevelt was a Martini man? The President who took the USA into World War Two was an enthusiast of the Dry Martini, regularly taking one or two before dinner. Whether he developed his taste before or after the abolition of Prohibition will probably never be known, although he later claimed that he had mixed the first ever legal Martini in the White House.

Despite all he did to improve the lives of drinkers in America, Roosevelt has never quite earned the approval of the true Martini aficionado. This is because he had a tendency to add offbeat ingredients such as anisette and fruit juice to spice up his Martinis. For the Martini purist, that simply isn't done.

WOMEN'S LIBERATION

After the repeal of Prohibition, the bars of America re-opened their doors to a very different clientele. In the days of the saloon bar, no respectable lady would have dared to be seen in those dens of iniquity and expect to emerge with her reputation intact. But, by 1933, the suffrage movement had brought a certain amount of equality between the sexes. In fact, the change of law allowing women the vote was passed just six months after the law that had introduced Prohibition.

The speakeasies had become popular haunts for women during the dry days of Prohibition. They were ideal places to socialize, to flirt and to dance, to see and be seen. Dresses became looser, hemlines crept higher and there was a boom in the sale and use of cosmetics.

BIRTH OF THE COCKTAIL LOUNGE

With alcohol once again deregulated, bars began to capitalize on the increased public for their wares. Bar-owners were more than happy to supply safe, sophisticated drinking places for their customers. Music, ambience and service were the order of the day. Although in some states of America there were specific laws that prohibited women from being served at the bar, these were circumvented by installing tables and booths with waiter service. The cocktail lounge

Talk of the town: flapper Doris Kenyon receives a toast from the other women in the cast of **The Half-way Girl** *(1924).*

was born. Gin continued to be the most popular alcoholic beverage in America, and the Martini flourished once more.

Café Rouge With the whole world swinging to the Big Band sound, many bars achieved an international reputation. One such venue was the Café Rouge Ballroom at the Hotel Pennsylvania in Manhattan, which hosted such famous names as Count Basie, Duke Ellington and, most notably, the Glenn Miller Orchestra. Miller later immortalized the ballroom with his 1938 hit 'Pennsylvania 6–5000', the title of which was derived from the hotel's telephone number.

VEGAS!

In 1941, Tommy Hull opened the El Rancho Hotel Casino in a small, isolated town in the Nevada Desert. The town was called Las Vegas,

and the El Rancho was the first of the luxury resort hotels that were to transform the former shanty town into the glittering gambling capital of the world. Las Vegas had been one of the few places in America left virtually untouched by the Great Depression. There was almost no unemployment in town during the 1930s, because most of the working population had been hired either to help complete the Union Pacific railway line through Nevada or to build the nearby Hoover Dam. And there was a third source of employment in town: gambling.

In 1931, the Nevada Legislature had legalized gambling in the state. Tired of trying to clamp down on all the backroom gambling joints that were flourishing to keep the local workers amused, they decided it was better to join them than to try to beat them. With any form of gambling still outlawed in the surrounding states, Las Vegas

Bar none: a typical 1950s cocktail lounge.

Three's company: Stalin, Roosevelt and Churchill at the Tehran Conference in 1943.

became a magnet for fun-seekers from all around America and the locals were happy to tend to their every need.

Sniffing easy money, other entrepreneurs began to arrive. The main road through Las Vegas – the Los Angeles Highway, later to be renamed The Strip – became the epicentre of a construction storm. Vegas was a boom town, only the prospectors brought the gold into the town rather than vice versa. The Martini had found a new home.

THE MARTINI GOES TO WAR

In 1943, a summit meeting was called between the war leaders Franklin D. Roosevelt, Winston Churchill and Joseph Stalin. The venue was the Russian Embassy in Tehran. The main item on the agenda was how to unify the American, British and Russian forces against Adolf Hitler. In the spirit of camaraderie, Roosevelt opened the meeting by mixing one of his special Dirty Martinis for his companions. These cocktails comprised two parts gin to one part vermouth, with a shot of olive brine.

Churchill's response has been lost to posterity but, given that he had once said that the perfect Martini entailed passing the cork from a vermouth bottle over a glass of gin, he was probably unimpressed. While Stalin proved more forthcoming, he had his reservations. He described the drink as 'all right, but it is cold in the stomach'.

POSTWAR CELEBRATIONS

If the years of World War Two gave much of the western world cause for sober reflection, it was soon back to business as usual. On VE Day, the party resumed. In Europe, this meant slowly rebuilding the distilleries that had been destroyed by the advancing German army. The Nazis had raided the factories and melted down all the copper stills and piping in order to make gun casings.

There was good news for the Martini, however. New, improved filtration processes developed by the distilleries now allowed gin to be produced without its trademark yellow colouration. For the first time, the Martini could be mixed with crystal clarity. The famous ode 'A Drink With Something In It' by Ogden Nash is all we have to remind us that the old-style Martini did not get its colour from the olive:

There is something about a Martini,

A tingle remarkably pleasant;

A yellow, mellow Martini;

I wish I had one at present.

There is something about a Martini,

Ere the dining and dancing begin,

And to tell you the truth,

It's not the vermouth –

I think that perhaps it's the gin.

Smoky

ice cubes
¼ measure dry vermouth
2 measures gin
1 measure sloe gin
  (see page 94)
5 drops of orange bitters
orange twist

A single measure of sloe gin adds a wonderful flavour to a traditional Martini. You can buy sloe gin ready-made or make your own.

Put the ice cubes into a mixing glass, add the vermouth and stir until the ice cubes are well coated. Pour in the gin, sloe gin and orange bitters and stir well, then strain into a chilled cocktail glass and add an orange twist.

Ernest Hemingway enjoys a Martini with his third wife, **Martha Gelhorn.**

THE MONTGOMERY

Ernest Hemingway's Martini was nicknamed a Montgomery, after the famous British field marshal. Monty was reputed to favour odds of 15 to 1 on the battlefield, and thus Hemingway's beloved Montgomeries were composed of 15 measures of gin to 1 of vermouth

'I had never tasted anything so cool and clean. They made me feel civilized.'

Ernest Hemingway describing the Martini in A Farewell to Arms (1929).

Opal Martini

This is the original fruity cocktail, with the taste of the fresh orange juice emphasized by the intense and powerful orange flavour of the Cointreau.

ice cubes
2 measures gin
1 measure Cointreau
2 measures fresh orange
  juice
orange twist

Put the ice cubes, gin, Cointreau and orange juice into a cocktail shaker and shake well. Strain into a chilled cocktail glass. Drape a long twist of orange rind in the drink and around the stem of the glass in a swirl. Serve immediately.

GANGSTERS INVADE VEGAS

World War Two had been good news for criminals. Having seen their profits take a tumble after the lifting of Prohibition, the mobsters had turned to various forms of extortion, gambling and narcotics smuggling to make ends meet. The war years proved to be a boon for the major crime syndicates. Presiding over a huge black market in consumer goods, they began to exert an influence over every aspect of American life.

In the early 1940s, the glamorous gangster Benjamin 'Bugsy' Siegel decided to muscle in on Las Vegas. After attempting hostile takeovers of various hotel casinos, Siegel eventually settled on the Flamingo Hotel and made owner Billy Wilkerson an offer he couldn't refuse. Siegel was hired as Wilkerson's 'assistant', but essentially took over the business through a campaign of terror and intimidation. Under his inept rule, however, the Flamingo fell heavily into debt and, eventually, someone put a bullet into Bugsy. Yet his instincts had been right: Las Vegas was made for the Mob.

The casinos provided an effective way of laundering money accrued from more dubious ventures. The presence of gangsters did little to tarnish the image of the town either. If anything, they added spice to Vegas's 'anything goes' reputation. Little by little, the big names opened up along The Strip: The Desert Inn (later to become the home of the millionaire recluse Howard Hughes), The Sands Hotel (the notorious stomping-ground of the Rat Pack), the Luxor, Circus Circus and, perhaps the most famous of all, Caesar's Palace.

DECLINE IN THE FIFTIES

Although the Martini remained a mainstay of the cocktail scene throughout the 1950s, it faced some serious competition. American GIs returning from Hawaii and the South Pacific at the end of the war had brought back tales of exotic drinks sipped on sun-drenched beaches in the company of sultry Polynesian maidens. This led to a brief fad for the Tiki lounge: exotic bars decked out in palm trees and faux ethnic ornaments, with island music drifting through the air and drinks like the Piña Colada, the Chi-Chi and the Zombie on the menu.

Whereas previously world travel had been the domain of the well-heeled, the sudden boom in tourism and cheap passenger airlines meant that more and more people were vacationing abroad and sampling foreign liquor. They brought their new-found wisdom back with them and spread the word. Bartenders were more than happy to adopt kitschy 'themes' for their bars and to experiment with unusual ingredients and ever more exotic drinks. Many of these left the Martini looking rather drab and staid.

Cocktails in the Home There was another threat to traditional American drinking establishments. Bars were having a hard time competing with a new breed of drinker being targeted by drinks manufacturers – the 'nuclear family'. Aware that the newly affluent young families of America preferred the joys of hearth and home, companies began to promote the benefits of do-it-yourself cocktails, offering mix kits, shakers and glasses, recipe books and all the trimmings at an affordable price. Why go out to a stuffy old bar when you could mix these tasty treats in your very own kitchen to enjoy with family and friends?

Advertising also began targeting younger and younger drinkers, who were able to circumvent age restrictions more easily if they knocked together cocktails at home. Anyway, with their polite atmosphere, sombre rituals and old-fashioned entertainment, traditional cocktail lounges just weren't cool.

DISSENTING VOICES

The Martini was also coming under fire from the media. The crusading journalist Westbrook Pegler cautioned: 'More people get their glasses broken and arrested and divorced on account of Martinis than for any other reason.' In 1952, the *New York Times* bemoaned the 'dumbing-down' of society with this reprimand: 'Along every stretch of polished mahogany in public places and in countless living rooms, there is no talk of the world crisis ... only of how to get a Martini *really* dry.'

No less a figure than Russian premier Nikita Khrushchev fired a salvo during the Cold War when he declared that the humble Martini was 'the USA's most lethal weapon'.

THE VODKA MARTINI

The early 1960s were a time of flux in America. They saw the Cuban missile crisis and the Cold War, Martin Luther King and the move towards racial integration, the assassinations of John F. Kennedy and his brother Robert, and the Vietnam War and the rise of the protest movement. Each of these social upheavals pointed towards a fundamental change in thinking and a rejection of old-style values.

As society made a seismic shift, so did the Martini. For the first time in half a century, gin was supplanted as the spirit of choice in America – by vodka. It was ironic that a Russian drink should become America's favourite tipple when the Cold War was at its height and patriots were expected to adhere to the credo that they were 'better dead than red'.

Shaken, Not Stirred Exactly how much we can thank author Ian Fleming for the rise in popularity of vodka is debatable. In 1953, the former journalist published *Casino Royale*.

TOP-CLASS ENTERTAINMENT

The Las Vegas cocktail lounges and ballrooms could afford to attract big showbiz names to entertain their guests as they sipped their Martinis. Frank Sinatra, Dean Martin and the rest of the Rat Pack made the Copa Room in Vegas their second home. Don Rickles, Buddy Hackett and Louis Prima were stars in Vegas long before the rest of the world had ever heard of them. Even Elvis Presley triumphantly relaunched his career there in 1969.

Vesper

ice cubes
3 measures gin
1 measure vodka
½ measure Lillet (see page 94)
lemon twist

This cocktail, made with a combination of gin and vodka, is prepared by James Bond's method – in other words it is shaken, not stirred.

Put the ice cubes, gin, vodka and Lillet into a cocktail shaker and shake well. Strain into a chilled cocktail glass and add a lemon twist.

Cosmopolitan

The first neo-tini, dating from the mid 1990s, this is a perfect combination of fresh fruity flavours.

ice cubes
1½ measures citron vodka, such as Absolut
1 measure Cointreau
1½ measures cranberry juice
¼ measure fresh lime juice
flamed orange twist (see page 94)

Put the ice cubes into a cocktail shaker, add the citron vodka, Cointreau, cranberry juice and lime juice and shake well. Strain into a chilled cocktail glass and add a flamed orange twist.

Sake-tini

ice cubes
2½ measures sake
1 measure vodka
½ measure orange Curaçao
2 thin cucumber wheels

Japan's best-known drink, sake, is fermented from rice. Here, along with orange Curaçao, it gives a Vodkatini a beautifully aromatic edge.

Put the ice cubes into a mixing glass, add the sake, vodka and Curaçao and stir well. Strain into a chilled cocktail glass and add two cucumber wheels, made by peeling the cucumber in strips, lengthwise and then thinly slicing.

This introduced the world to the suave British secret service agent James Bond. In that book, agent 007 provided a recipe for his favourite drink: a Vesper shaken, not stirred.

While Fleming's books proved popular throughout the 1950s – JFK let slip that *From Russia With Love* was his all-time favourite novel, and there had been a television adaptation of *Casino Royale* as early as 1954 – it wasn't until the arrival of actor Sean Connery in the very first Bond movie, *Dr No*, in 1962, that the character really took off. Here, Bond's tipple had been simplified to a Vodka Martini, a Vodkatini (see page 36). It swiftly became the order of the day in bars both across America and around the world.

Spy master: author Ian Fleming.

THE DEATH OF THE MARTINI?

In 1976, US presidential candidate Jimmy Carter delivered a keynote speech during his election campaign in which he railed against corporate fat cats who indulged in 'three Martini lunches' on expense accounts. He considered such behaviour an affront to the decent taxpayer. Carter had some very vocal opposition, but he had the last laugh. He won the election.

Whether intentional or not, Carter had caught the spirit of the age. Previously the epitome of all that was cool and stylish, the Martini had now become synonymous with over-indulgence.

YOUTH REBELLION

In a 1973 article in *Esquire* magazine, food writer James Villas railed against drinkers who deliberately set out to get drunk, and considered the Martini to blame: 'Generally, the Martini signifies absolute decadence. Specifically, it means a bitter, medicinal-tasting beverage. It stands for everything from phony bourgeois values and social snobbery to jaded alcoholism and latent masochism ... Young people do not like Martinis and they're not drinking them. Ever! Anywhere!'

Villas was half right. Young people certainly weren't drinking Martinis any more. But this was less a rejection of 'bourgeois values and social snobbery' than a more fundamental form of rebellion. Drinking Martinis was no longer considered cool. Martinis were what your parents drank. There were far more effective ways for youths to get up the noses of authority figures, whether it be through cheap booze, soft drugs or simply antisocial music. In any case, during the global financial recession of the 1970s, who could afford cocktails?

For anyone caught between teenage years and middle age – the twenty- and thirtysomethings – hard liquor was also on the wane.

The whole world was on a health kick, eating macrobiotic food and drinking bottled water. If you were going to drink, the tendency was towards lighter drinks like wine or beer.

Slowly and with little fanfare, the Martini seemed to be on its way out. But it turned out that the Martini hadn't died – it was merely resting.

THE MODERN MARTINI

In 1985, *Time* magazine published an article describing the Martini as 'an amusing antique'. Yet, after a decade of neglect, the Martini was poised to stage a triumphant comeback. Much of this was dictated by fashion. With the 1950s retro look very much in vogue, the Martini became an essential accessory. It was hard to look cool in your cocktail dress or lounge suit unless you had a suitable drink in your hand. If you were balancing a big, fat Havana cigar in the other, so much the better.

Another critical factor was the rise of the upwardly mobile businessperson, who wanted to work hard and play harder – the 'masters of the universe', the 'city kids' and their ilk. With a huge disposable income at their fingertips, the pricey cocktail bars were no longer beyond their reach and provided a useful social barometer to measure the level of their success.

Tastes had also changed in modern times as wine and beer were now deemed boring. The youth of the 1980s and 1990s had rediscovered their thirst for exotica. As the pioneering marketing consultant and style guru Faith Popcorn saw it: 'The Martini may again be popular because self-indulgence has replaced self-denial as the reigning fashion.' This is just another way of saying that the Martini drinkers of today aren't so different from their counterparts in the 1920s.

MARTINIGATE

According to popular legend, the disgraced American President Richard Nixon (pictured above right with Charles Rebozo) was drowning his sorrows in Martinis when he was driven from office after the Watergate scandal. On that evening, Nixon was being consoled by Charles 'Bebe' Rebozo, a wealthy Florida banker and businessman. 'Bebe' was one of Nixon's staunchest drinking buddies, and he later confided that 'Tricky Dicky' favoured the classic 'In and Out' Martini: pour the vermouth and ice into the shaker, swing it round once and empty it before adding the gin. Proportions were a stout 7 measures of gin to 1 of vermouth.

'A Vodka Martini.
Shaken, not stirred.'

James Bond

**The Domino principle: Sean Connery as James Bond and Claudine Auger
as Domino Vitali in Thunderball (1965).**

Vodkatini

**¼ measure dry vermouth
3 measures frozen vodka
2 green olives or
  lemon twist**

Vodka is used instead of gin in this classic recipe. Vodkatinis are usually served very dry.

*Swirl the vermouth around a chilled Martini glass then pour in the vodka. Finish
by adding the olives or a lemon twist.*

Polish Martini

ice cubes
1 measure Zubrowka vodka
(see page 95)
1 measure Krupnik vodka
(see page 94)
1 measure Wyborowa
vodka (standard Polish)
1 measure apple juice
lemon twist

This is a wonderfully mellow Martini made with three different types of Polish vodka with traditional honey and bison grass flavours.

Put the ice cubes into a mixing glass. Pour in the three vodkas and the apple juice and stir well. Strain into a chilled cocktail glass and add a lemon twist.

Martini Mixology

When it comes to mixing Martinis, it's all a matter of taste. Some Martini 'snobs' insist that only infinitesimally precise measurements will do, that certain arcane rituals must be religiously observed during mixing and that particular ingredients and garnishes are absolutely forbidden. Take no notice. It's *your* drink. You can mix and drink your Martini however you like.

BASIC INGREDIENTS

Gin Anyone who has ever perused the gin section of their local liquor store will know that there is a bewildering array on offer: London gin, Plymouth gin, Old Tom gin, American gin. You may even have come across bottles of old-style genever.

Old Tom gin is a sweetened variety that has its roots in 18th-century London. Some public houses that sold the drink advertised with a specially crafted sign featuring a tom cat – a coin placed in the cat's mouth would allow the drinker to suck a shot of gin through a tube. Genever continues to be produced in numerous European countries, as it has been for centuries. Genever is closer to whiskey than modern gin and tends to be yellowish in colour with a distinctively aromatic flavour, making it less than ideal for a Dry Martini. Unless you are setting out to replicate the original Martinez cocktail created in 19th-century America, you'd be advised to steer clear of both Old Tom gin and any form of genever.

The British styles of dry gin tend to be the most popular for the making of Martinis, which means either London gin or Plymouth gin. Choosing between them is really down to personal preference, although Plymouth gin is generally more fruity and aromatic. American gins are also fine for Martinis, although they are far less potent than their British counterparts and, to some palates, less flavourful. Even in America, most bartenders stick to London Dry.

Vermouth Vermouth is available in sweet, dry and extra dry varieties. Sweet red vermouth will give your Martini a distinctly pinkish hue. It's probably best to stick with white vermouth and let your taste buds decide how sweet or dry you prefer it.

'Do not allow children to mix drinks. It is unseemly and they use too much vermouth.'

Steve Allen

MARASCHINO AND ORANGE BITTERS

Although the original Martinez cocktail called for the addition of both Maraschino and orange bitters, these are no longer considered to be staple ingredients of the Martini. By the beginning of the 20th century, most recipes had dropped the Maraschino. The bitters were the last to go, although some bartenders still included a shot of them well into the 1920s and some aficionados swear by them even today. If you are feeling experimental, you could always try reintegrating some of these 'lost' ingredients and see what you think.

Exotic Variations All of the tips above apply to the gin-based Dry Martini (see page 9). Throughout this book, you'll also find recipes for exotic varieties of the drink, each of which demand additional ingredients. These will be explained along with the details of preparation in the relevant recipe.

THE RIGHT EQUIPMENT

If you are serious about your Martini mixing, you might consider investing in a set of Martini glasses and your own cocktail shaker.

Martini Glasses A Martini undoubtedly tastes more satisfying when sipped from an elegant Martini glass. This is partly due to the design. The long stem helps to keep the drink cold by not allowing the warmth of the drinker's hand to come into contact with the bowl of the glass. The wide brim of the glass reputedly increases surface tension, which brings out the full bouquet of the drink.

Cocktail Shakers While it is possible to shake a Martini in an old jamjar if necessary, proper cocktail shakers come in such a wide variety of funky shapes and styles as to be almost irresistible. You could even try scouring around antique shops and flea markets to see if you can unearth one of the classic shakers from the 1930s through to the 1960s. Be warned, though, that vintage shakers are eminently collectable and can come with a hefty price tag.

Other Essentials For measuring liquids, it is best either to buy a set of shot glasses – they always come in useful for other cocktails – or to use a proper spirit measure. A long-handled spoon is also essential if you are planning to have your Martinis stirred, not shaken. Last but not least, don't forget the cocktail sticks.

EVOLUTION OF THE MARTINI GLASS

The identity of the inventor of the Martini glass is as much a mystery as that of the originator of the drink itself. One popular version of events leads us to Antoine Peychaurd, a French apothecary who emigrated to New Orleans and opened a pharmacy.

Although Antoine dispensed prescriptions and remedies during the day, at night he busied himself with a very different type of medicine. Close friends were invited into his back room, where he would mix up various alcoholic beverages. For this he used a small device for measuring prescriptions called a *coquetier*, which is the French word for egg cup.

Over the years, and with a little help from the tongue-twisting effects of Peychaurd's potent concoctions, 'coquetier' gradually metamorphosed into 'cocktail'.

CLASSIC GARNISHES

A Martini isn't a Martini without that subtle hint of colour offered by its garnish. These days, it is unthinkable to drink a Martini without an olive. However, it was not always so. In terms of the history of the Martini, the olive was something of a Johnny-come-lately. The Martinis being mixed in the early part of the 20th century were invariably garnished with either a twist of lemon or a cocktail cherry.

Olives The olive only put in an appearance in the 1920s, when Martinis were becoming increasingly dry and more susceptible to the bitterness of the olive. Who first popped an olive into their drink is anyone's guess. It has even been suggested that olives first appeared when the cocktail began being mixed in London and that they were only subsequently adopted by American bartenders.

So what type of olive should you use? It's a matter of taste.

White Elephant

Simple and smooth, the blend of vodka and crème de caçao – a white chocolate liqueur – gives this creamy cocktail a powerful punch. It is served without a decoration.

ice cubes
1½ measures vodka
1 measure white crème de caçao
1 measure single cream
½ measure full-cream milk

Put the ice cubes into a cocktail shaker, add the vodka, crème de cacao, cream and milk and shake thoroughly. Strain into a chilled Martini glass.

Mood music: Joan Crawford with a Martini in Humoresque (1946).

'Happiness is a Dry Martini and a good woman ... or a bad woman.'

George Burns

Vochacino

ice cubes
1½ measures vodka
½ measure Toussaint (see page 95)
½ measure sugar syrup (see page 95)
1 measure double cream
½ shot espresso coffee
chocolate syrup
cocoa powder, to decorate

Several distinctly different elements – vodka, mocha and cappucino – combine to make this a particularly delicious cocktail.

Put the ice cubes into a cocktail shaker, pour in the vodka, Toussaint, sugar syrup, double cream and espresso coffee. Decorate the inside of a chilled glass with a rough spiral of chocolate syrup. Shake the drink thoroughly then strain into the glass and decorate with a sprinkling of cocoa powder.

'If the Lord hadn't intended us to have a
three Martini lunch, then why do you suppose
He put all those olive trees in the Holy Land?'

House Speaker Jim Wright

Traditionally, an olive stuffed with pimento is the garnish of choice, with the pepper adding a tiny flash of red to the drink. However, plain olives are fine, too – just be careful not to crack your teeth on the stone! For the more adventurous, you could try one of the more exotic types of cocktail olives, such as those stuffed with anchovies, blue cheese or almonds.

Other Garnishes Many people just can't stand the taste of olives. So don't feel embarrassed about asking for a twist of lemon or cherry instead. Or try a caper, a slice of ginger, a pistachio nut, a cherry tomato or a wedge of cucumber.

Gaining popularity in America, too, is the 'tomolive' – a small, green plum or grape tomato that has been cooked and subsequently pickled. This unusual garnish combines the classic colour of an olive with the sharp sweetness of a tomato, making it palatable to those who dislike olives.

ICE COOL

Few things taste quite so unpleasant as a warm Martini. On the other hand, though, a watery Martini can be just as bad. So, when it comes to correctly chilling your Martini, it is critical that the ice is not allowed to melt and thus dilute the drink.

The best way to ensure this is not to let the ice stand in the open air while you are mixing your drinks. Take it straight from the freezer and put it into the cocktail shaker, pour in the vermouth and gin immediately, shake or stir, and strain the liquid into the glass. Then throw away the ice. It may take some practice, but what you are trying to ensure is that the gin, vermouth and ice are in contact in the shaker for long enough to chill the liquid, but not so long that the ice begins to melt and fuse with the alcohol.

Some true Martini aficionados also suggest storing your gin, Martini shaker and glasses in the freezer, so that they are also completely chilled through (don't try to freeze the vermouth – it'll turn rock solid). Whether you choose to follow their advice is up to you ... and the size of your freezer!

A Martini is meant to be enjoyed at the moment of mixing, not saved for later. So resist the urge to store Martinis in the fridge.

'The best Martini will be the coldest Martini.'

Barnaby Conrad III

The Gibson

Question: When is a Martini not a Martini?
Answer: When it's a Gibson.

For the strict Martini purist, their favourite tipple is mixed with an almost religious fervour. Measures may vary from taste bud to taste bud, but all are agreed that the definitive Martini is composed of nothing more than gin, vermouth and an olive. So, · if you should happen to prefer a small cocktail onion in your drink rather than an olive, it isn't a Martini but a Gibson.

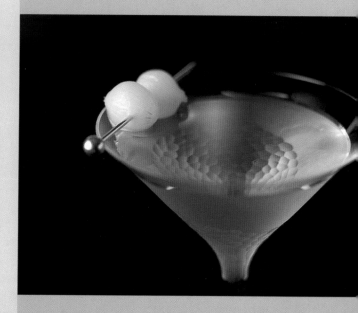

'You can no more keep a Martini in the refrigerator than you can keep a kiss there. The proper union of gin and vermouth is one of the happiest marriages on Earth, and one of the shortest lived.'

Bernard de Voto

SWEET OR DRY?

So you have all your ingredients. The ice is rock hard. Your thirst is waiting to be quenched. You're ready to start mixing.

If you're a complete Martini novice, it's a good idea to start with what is generally agreed to be the classic measurements for a Dry Martini (see the recipe on page 9). If you find the ratio either too dry or too sweet, it's easy to adjust it to suit your particular palate. If it is too sweet, simply increase the dryness by adding more gin. If you feel it's too dry, increase the amount of vermouth. It's as simple as that.

A USEFUL TIP

Some bartenders maintain that adding a single drop of whiskey to a Martini helps take away the initial astringency one feels with the first sip. The whiskey has the effect of making the Martini far smoother and rounder. This isn't of much use, though, if you happen to like that first 'sting' of a freshly prepared Martini on your lips and tongue.

Don't be afraid to experiment until you find the balance of ingredients that you prefer. There are no rules as to how sweet or dry a Martini should be – some bartenders even suggest that it is sufficient to simply let a ray of sunlight shine through a bottle of vermouth and onto a glass of gin to get the requisite dryness (although it has to be said that the drink resulting from this particular recipe might more accurately be described as a glass of cold gin rather than a Martini).

SHAKEN OR STIRRED?

According to the great British author W. Somerset Maugham, a Martini should be stirred. However, restaurateur Curtis Post of the Occidental Grill in San Francisco begs to differ: 'You've got to shake until your hand hurts. When you pour, it's so cold the glass looks like a miniature blizzard inside.' Everyone knows James Bond's thoughts on the subject. So should a Martini be shaken or stirred? Does it even make a difference?

Stirring The argument in favour of stirring is put forward by those who feel that the clarity of the Martini is all important. A stirred Martini sits crystal clear in the glass, whereas a shaken Martini has a slightly cloudy quality on account of the shattered ice fragments that settle on the surface.

Shaking Those in favour of a shaken Martini claim that the shaking action 'bruises' the gin, which releases its full aromatic flavour. This effect can also, it has been said, be achieved by 'chop-stirring' the drink – stirring in a vigorous up-and-down movement rather than clockwise.

MYTHS AND GIMMICKS

If the results published by the Royal Society of Chemistry (see below) would seem to disprove the theoretical differences between shaking and stirring – and there were any number of Martini drinkers who

'A Martini should always be stirred, not shaken, so that the molecules lie sensuously on top of one another.'

W. Somerset Maugham

Mixmasters: bar staff at London's Embassy Club in 1933.

SCIENTIFIC EVIDENCE

Is there any real scientific proof that shaking or stirring fundamentally affects the taste of the Martini? In 2002, the Royal Society of Chemistry in London decided to conduct an experiment. They planned to shake and stir Martinis under laboratory conditions and see whether they could scientifically calibrate the difference between the two methods. In their published report, they claimed that shaking or stirring resulted in no appreciable difference in taste. However, because the shaking brought more of the alcohol into direct contact with the ice, the shaken Martini was significantly colder than the stirred Martini.

wrote in to complain that their experiment was flawed – there are numerous other myths and legends about Martinis that can more easily be dismissed. Such as the American bartender who claimed he had isolated the vermouth molecule and could thus adjust the dryness of his Martinis on a molecular level.

Lots of gimmicks and gadgets have been introduced to Martini mixing, the usefulness of which is debatable, such as the calibrated Martini dropper invented by Hammacher Schlemmer. One bartender even insists on finely spraying the vermouth onto the surface of his Martinis using an atomizer.

In 1961, the Autobar division of the American Machine and Metals Corporation devised an automatic Martini vending machine. Called the Cocktailmatic, it repeatedly dispensed a perfectly-mixed Martini at the push of a button and was aimed at the cocktail enthusiasts mixing drinks at home.

MOOD MUSIC

To appreciate a good Martini, you need the right ambience. If mixing your Martinis at home, close the curtains, dim the lights and put on some suitable music.

Easy Listening The recent revival of interest in cocktail culture has prompted music companies to rediscover some long-deleted albums of lounge music. Many obscure 'easy listening' records from the 1950s and 1960s are now available once more on CD.

Cool Jazz You certainly can't go wrong with some tasteful jazz floating through the air. You could try the sublime John Coltrane or perhaps some early Miles Davis. Dave Brubeck, George Shearing,

Special delivery: news reporter George McEvoy demonstrates the Cocktailmatic automated Martini dispenser.

Spinning discs: choose a selection of music from the suggestions below to help you create the perfect Martini.

Stan Getz and early Gerry Mulligan should also make for a perfect Martini moment. Or maybe one of the soundtrack albums by the perennially cool John Barry.

Mellow Ballads Virtually anything by the veteran crooners Frank Sinatra, Dean Martin or Tony Bennett should mix well with your Martinis – as will the vocal stylings of Mel Torme or Julie London. Their nearest contemporary equivalent would probably be the singer Harry Connick Jr.

Music for Love If you are planning a romantic evening, Burt Bacharach should set the mood nicely, as should Serge Gainsbourg, who is probably most famous for 'Je t'aime ... moi non plus'. Or try Jimmy Webb's 'Ten Easy Pieces' album, on which the songwriter strips down his most famous songs into elegant solo piano numbers.

Modern Sounds There are lots of modern artists dedicated to the fine art of chilling out. Worthy of investigation are 'Moon Safari' by French electro-pop duo Air, the neo-soundtrack music of Goldfrapp on the album 'Felt Mountain', 'Play' by the quirky cut-and-mix master Moby, and Massive Attack's 'Mezzanine' album.

THE PERFECT MIX

Everyone has their own idea about the measures for the perfect tipple. President Franklin D. Roosevelt reputedly favoured a relatively innocuous two parts gin to one part vermouth, while Ernest Hemingway preferred a teeth-gritting fifteen parts gin to one part vermouth, known as the Montgomery (see page 28). Your ideal Martini will probably lie somewhere between these two extremes.

Happy hours: Eli Wallach and Dean Martin share a Martini in How to Save a Marriage (and Ruin Your Life) *in 1968.*

Martinis in the Movies

If the Martini had not existed, Hollywood would probably have had to invent it. Martinis have been present in movies since the very dawn of the silent cinema. They have been used as a symbol of rebellion, of sophistication and of utter decadence. They have been sipped, gulped, spilled and thrown in people's faces. Indeed, we have become so used to seeing certain actors and characters with a Martini glass in their hand that, without one, they are somehow rendered incomplete.

You can almost lose count of the number of actors immortalized in drink, with cocktails named after Douglas Fairbanks, Mary Pickford, Ginger Rogers, Jean Harlow, Lupe Velez and Marlene Dietrich, to name but a few. Pint-sized Shirley Temple even had a special non-alcoholic cocktail named in her honour.

Seldom has there been a more versatile prop for an actor. Not for nothing has it become part of Hollywood folklore that, even to present times, the very final camera set-up in each day's filming schedule is known as 'the Martini shot'.

Yet, if the Martini has become a ubiquitous presence in the movies, it has not been without a struggle. The forces of censorship have vigorously campaigned against it, citing it as a corrupting influence on the viewing public. As far back as 1916, the National Association of the Motion Picture Industry – Hollywood's first ever self-censorship committee – was trying to get film-makers to clean up their acts, including on-screen displays of drinking. Not that film-makers ever paid the slightest bit of attention to them. They simply found ways round NAMPI's edicts.

SILENT MOVIE

In 1928, cinema audiences were flocking to see a new silent comedy starring screen superstar Mary Astor. Its title was *Dry Martini*. How could a film with such a provocative title be released during the height of Prohibition? Simple. It was set in Paris. The American

Continental drift: the American cast of Dry Martini (1928) avoid the woes of Prohibition by whooping it up in Paris, France.

Venus in furs: the incomparable Mae West in Goin' to Town (1935).

government might well be able to legislate over the behaviour of its own citizens, but it had absolutely no control over anything that happened in the fleshpots of Gay Paree.

However, just to be on the safe side, director Harry D'Abbadie D'Arrast ensured that *Dry Martini* had a moral ... of sorts. The film revolves around a divorced American expatriate, Willoughby Quimby (Albert Gran), who is living the high life in Paris. Discovering that his daughter Elizabeth (Mary Astor) is arriving to pay him a visit, he is forced to give up his daily intake of booze and loose women so as not to set a bad example. Elizabeth, however, is not quite the paragon of virtue her father believes her to be and, bored by his abstemious lifestyle, allows herself to be whisked off her feet by a raffish artist (Albert Conti), only belatedly realizing his true nature. Her father eventually manages to marry Elizabeth off to one of his less nefarious friends (Matt Moore), before blissfully settling back into his former dissolute lifestyle.

Censorship By the time *Dry Martini* hit cinemas around America, the National Association of the Motion Picture Industry had been replaced by the Motion Pictures Producers and Distributors of America. This was yet another self-censorship board, which operated under the eagle-eyed presidency of Will Hays, the former US Postmaster General. Not only did the organization censor each and every film, they also had the power to veto screenplays before they even reached the screen. Among their list of 13 elements that should never be depicted on screen

`... three Martinis under his belt and a full wallet in his pocket.'

Mae West describing the prerequisites of her ideal man

was anything which 'made gambling and drunkenness attractive'.

Yet there was one Martini enthusiast who was going to give the MPPDA a run for its money. Her name was Mae West.

MAE WEST

In the vaudeville theatre of the 1920s, Mae West's breezy attitude towards her libido, and her salacious way with a *double entendre*, had transformed such self-penned theatrical extravaganzas as *Diamond Lil* and *Sex* into huge hits. Not that any of this stopped the authorities from trying to close her down the moment she walked on stage. In 1925, she was thrown in jail for a week after police raided the theatre showing *Sex*. Another show, *The Pleasure Man*, lasted just two performances.

Given West's reputation, it was only a matter of time before Hollywood came calling. In 1932, she made her screen debut opposite George Raft in the film *Night After Night*. Although she was making little more than a cameo appearance, West had insisted on rewriting all her own dialogue, including the immortal riposte to a hat check girl, who says admiringly of her jewellery: 'Goodness, what lovely diamonds!' 'Goodness had nothing to do with it, dearie,' fired back West, all but winking at the camera. For the audience, it was love at first soundbite.

Clashing with the Censors If cinema-goers were delighted by West's loose tongue and even looser morals, the censors were mortified. When, in 1933, she began making plans to bring her stage triumph *Diamond Lil* to the screen, they put their foot down. The plot revolved around a lady saloon owner suspected of operating a white-slavery ring. When an undercover cop poses as a Salvation Army worker in order to crack the case, she not only proves her innocence but divests him of his in the process.

The censors had a field day. The most salacious dialogue was cut entirely. All references to white slavery were removed. There was to be no mention of the Salvation Army. Even the film's proposed setting of San Francisco's notorious Barbary Coast red-light district had to be changed to the Bowery in New York.

West Meets Grant None of the problems with the censors had the slightest effect on West's reputation as the nation's favourite bad girl. *She Done Him Wrong*, as *Diamond Lil* was renamed for the cinema, went on to become a huge hit and cemented her screen partnership with co-star Cary Grant.

Together, West and Grant rushed out another, equally successful, movie, *I'm No Angel* (1933). In that film, West even likened herself to her favourite drink. When asked how her character, Tira, had managed to get suckered into becoming involved with nefarious conman Slick Wiley (Ralf Harolde), she admits ruefully that she had been drawn into his schemes 'like an olive in a dry Martini'.

However, West was not the only Martini enthusiast to graduate from vaudeville to the silver screen. Her male couterpart was W.C. Fields.

W.C. FIELDS

The great comic actor W.C. Fields notoriously supplemented his breakfast with two Martinis, before mixing up a flask of chilled gin and vermouth to see him through the day's filming at the studio. He referred to the contents of his flask as his 'pineapple juice'. Legend also has it that Fields packed away up to two quarts of gin – or 'angel's milk', as he called it – a day.

Zoom

This is an unusual Martini made with a healthy slug of Scotch. It is served without a decoration so that the malt flavour can shine through..

ice cubes
2 measures blended
**   Scotch whisky**
1 teaspoon clear honey
1 measure chilled water
1 measure single cream

Put the ice cubes into a cocktail shaker, add the Scotch, honey, chilled water and single cream and shake well. Strain into an old-fashioned glass and serve at once.

Chocotini

Ice cubes
2 measures vodka
1 measure dark crème
**   de cacao**
¼ measure sugar syrup
**   (see page 95)**
½ measure chocolate
**   syrup (see page 94)**
cocoa powder, to
**   decorate**

This is much sweeter than a normal Martini, with rich, dark chocolate overtones.

Put the ice cubes into a cocktail shaker, add the vodka, creme de cacao, sugar and chocolate syrup and shake well. Strain into a chilled Martini glass that has been decorated with cocoa powder around the rim.

**Drunk driving: the irrepressible
W.C. Fields hits the road.**

Decatini

ice cubes
2 measures Stolichnaya
   Razberi (see page 95)
1 measure morello cherry
   purée (shop-bought)
½ measure chocolate syrup
   (see page 95)
½ measure double cream
chocolate syrup to
   decorate

The combination of raspberry, cherry, chocolate and double cream make a cocktail rather like a liquid slice of Black Forest gateau.

Fill a cocktail shaker with ice cubes and add the vodka, chocolate syrup and half of the cream. Shake well and strain into a chilled Martini glass. Shake the cherry purée with the rest of the cream in a clean shaker. Slowly pour the cherry liquid on to a spoon that is held in contact with the chocolate liquid in the glass; this will produce a layering effect. Decorate with a 'swirl' of chocolate syrup.

> '*I've been on a 46-year diet of olives and alcohol. The latter I consume. The former I save and use over again in more alcohol.*'

W.C. Fields

Fields' first film, *Pool Shark* (1915), was a simple recording of the popular stage act that he had been performing in vaudeville theatre since the end of the 19th century. In over a dozen films between the mid-1920s and 1930s, Fields developed his screen persona of a cynical misanthrope struggling in the face of a fickle universe. No one could play a drunk quite like Fields, possibly because he actually was drunk most of the time.

Fields was an unapologetic drinker. 'Twas a woman who drove me to drink, and I never had the courtesy to thank her for it', he once joked. Nor did his enthusiasm for the bottle wane even after his nose had exploded in florid gin blossoms. He once told an interviewer: 'I take inordinate pride in my nose. Indeed I have treatment done on it every day.' With this, he took another hearty swig of his 'treatment'.

MOBSTER MOVIES

If Mae West had caused the censors a headache, then another film genre which came of age in the 1930s was a full-blown migraine – the gangster movie. The rise of organized crime in the 1920s, particularly through its ties with the bootlegging industry and the speakeasies, had transformed one-time petty crooks and violent thugs into glamorous outlaws. Hollywood wasn't slow to recognize their potential as screen anti-heroes.

Mobsters dressed well, lived dangerous lives and rubbed shoulders with politicians and movie stars. The underworld teemed with illicit sex and casual violence – both of which were surefire draws at the box office. Every gangster's rise and fall had within it all of the elements required of high tragedy. Film-makers were happy to show it all: the speakeasies and the gin mills, the goodtime girls and the bad boys, the fast lives and the slow deaths.

The censors, needless to say, were up in arms. Despite protestations from film-makers that they were in no way condoning or glamorizing the exploits of criminals, but simply depicting the ugly facts of contemporary life, the censors weren't fooled. They knew that films such as *Little Caesar* (1931), *The Public Enemy* (1931) and, most notoriously, *Scarface* (1932) might well portray their title characters as sociopathic maniacs, but that did little to quell their fascination for cinema-goers.

George Raft You only have to look at the career of actor George Raft to see the appeal of the mobster in the eyes of the public. Raft was never much of an actor, yet he enjoyed a steady rise to stardom beginning in 1929 and escalating through the 1930s. Much of this was thanks to whispers about his alleged connections with the Mob.

The story goes that Raft had ties with the racketeers who had muscled in on the Hollywood labour unions. As a result, he was given a bit part in *Queen of the Night Clubs* (1929), opposite 'Texas' Guinan (see page 16), before graduating to bigger roles, invariably being cast as a mobster or heavy, in more prestigious movies.

Had he been forced to rely on his talents as an actor, it is likely that Raft would have sunk without trace. He was, at best, a wooden performer, with virtually no acting range and precious little screen presence. All he had going for him were his alleged 'connections' – he was rumoured to be big buddies with Benjamin 'Bugsy' Siegel, the glamorous gangster who conquered Hollywood and was, in turn, conquered by Las Vegas – but that was enough to guarantee him a career. People would go to his movies just to see what a genuine gangster looked like. Raft was canny enough neither to confirm nor to deny any of the rumours about his chequered past.

Lana Turner Hollywood's flirtation with organized crime was a lasting one. One of the most explosive incidents was the relationship between screen goddess Lana Turner and Johnny Stompanato, a former bodyguard to mobster Mickey Cohen. Their relationship was turbulent, with Stompanato repeatedly abusing Turner both mentally and physically. In 1958, Turner's daughter, Cheryl Crane, became so fearful of her mother's life that she stabbed Stompanato to death. In a final twist of irony, Turner emerged from this scandal and its subsequent court case an even bigger star than before. Her first film of the post-Stompanato era – *Imitation of Life* (1959) – was probably her biggest hit.

THE SURREAL MARTINI

The controversial Spanish surrealist film-maker Luis Buñuel claimed that 'to provoke, or sustain, a reverie in a bar, you have to drink English gin, especially in the form of the Dry Martini'. It was

BUÑUEL'S RECIPE

In his 1984 autobiography, My Last Breath, *Luis Buñuel (pictured above with actor Fernando Rey on the set of* That Obscure Object of Desire, *1977) presents his own recipe for the perfect Martini: 'The day before your guests arrive, put all the ingredients – glasses, gin and shaker – in the refrigerator. Use a thermometer to make sure the ice is about twenty degrees below zero (centigrade). Don't take anything out until your friends arrive; then pour a few drops of Noilly Prat and half a demitasse spoon of Angostura bitters over the ice. Shake it, then pour it out, keeping only the ice, which retains a faint taste of both. Then pour straight gin over the ice, shake it again, and serve.'*

during just such as reverie that Buñuel came up with a way to save his apparently doomed film *That Obscure Object of Desire* released in 1977.

Midway through the making of the film, Buñuel had a ferocious argument with the lead actress, as a result of which she left. With the loss of their only female star and no money with which to go back and reshoot all her scenes, Buñuel and producer Serge Silberman decided that they had no viable option but to abandon the film altogether. They retired to a nearby bar to drown their sorrows.

After a couple of Martinis, Buñuel suddenly had the brainwave of simply hiring another actress to complete the role. When the film was released, critics hailed it as a masterpiece and fell over themselves to praise Buñuel's brilliant and audacious scheme of having two entirely different women inhabit the same role, claiming it to be a triumph of the surrealist imagination rather than one of gin and vermouth.

A STAR IS BORN

By the time Prohibition was lifted in America in 1933, the Martini had already become a visible presence in the movies, being 'secretly' quaffed in speakeasies or other exotic locales. With the repeal of the Volstead Act, however, it assumed star status.

The Thin Man One of the first films to capitalize on the relaxing of the drinking laws was the 1933 comedy thriller *The Thin Man*, the first in a series of adventures for socialite sleuths Nick and Nora Charles, played by William Powell and Myrna Loy. The film was based on the novel by crime writer Dashiell Hammett, who knew a lot about detection – he had once been employed by the Pinkerton Detectives – and even more about booze. Nick and Nora were not the sort of people to let their detective work get in the way of their drinking, and were more often to be seen carrying a Martini glass than a magnifying glass. In the film, Nick even takes a break from the case to instruct a sloppy bartender on the fine art of cocktail mixing.

Mixed marriage: Cary Grant rustles up some Martinis in My Favourite Wife *(1940).*

William Powell and Maureen O'Sullivan share a Martini in the film The Thin Man *(1933).*

'You see, the important thing is the rhythm. You always have rhythm in your shaking. With a Manhattan, you shake to a foxtrot time. A Bronx to two-step time. A Dry Martini you always shake to waltz time.'

Nick Charles, played by William Powell, in The Thin Man

Mixing business with pleasure: Clark Gable and Constance Bennett in After Office Hours (1935).

Party Time
The party continued at full swing throughout the 1930s, and spilled over into the 1940s and 1950s.

Cary Grant continued to put all he had learned from Mae West into practice by downing Martinis in *When You're in Love* (1937) and *My Favourite Wife* (1940), although by *North by Northwest* in 1959 he had moved on to drinking Gibsons.

'Do you like gin? It's my only weakness,' admitted the sinister Dr Pretorius (Ernest Thesiger) in *Bride of Frankenstein* (1935).

'Let's all drink gin and make wry faces,' suggested Bob Hope helpfully in *The Cat and the Canary* (1937).

Ruthless news reporter Clark Gable romanced Constance Bennett over Martinis in *After Office Hours* (1935).

Even future US President Ronald Reagan could be seen plying dying socialite Bette Davis with Martinis in the classic melodrama *Dark Victory* (1939).

Joan Crawford drowned her sorrows in Martinis as the music patron devoted to violinist John Garfield in *Humoresque* (1946).

It seemed like all of Hollywood had gone Martini crazy.

Humphrey Bogart
'Of all the gin joints in all the towns in all the world, she walks into mine,' was the welcome that Rick Blaine (Humphrey Bogart) offered his beloved Ilsa (Ingrid Bergman) in the classic wartime weepie *Casablanca* (1942).

'The problem with the world is that everyone is a few drinks behind.'

Humphrey Bogart

Stars and bars: Gary Merrill joins Bette Davis for cocktails in **All About Eve** *(1950).*

Bogart would have been familiar with many of those 'gin joints'. As one of the legendary drinkers of the Golden Age of Hollywood, he and his wife Lauren Bacall had presided over the Holmby Hills Rat Pack, their private circle of drinking buddies. The Pack included Frank Sinatra, Judy Garland, Sid Luft, Swifty Lazar, Jimmy Van Heusen, Kay Thompson and David Niven. Niven also

once mixed one of the more memorable of the movies' Martinis as the long-suffering butler in the comedy *My Man Godfrey* in 1957.

While the irreplaceable Bogie has certainly earned his place in the history of the Martini, true aficionados will be unable to suppress a gasp at his dying words: 'I should never have switched from scotch to Martinis.'

Home comforts: Montgomery Clift and Donna Reed in From Here to Eternity (1953).

CLOUDS OF CONTROVERSY

'Fasten your seatbelts, it's gonna be a bumpy ride!' promised Bette Davis in *All About Eve* (1950), precariously balancing her Martini glass as she delivers the line. She wasn't wrong. Storm clouds were gathering over Hollywood, prompted by director Fred Zinnemann's decision to film an adaptation of James Jones's World War Two novel *From Here to Eternity*. The book caused controversy when published in 1951 for its portrayal of military life, complete with brothels, adulterous affairs and profane dialogue.

When they looked at the script, the Motion Picture Association of America (formerly the MPPDA) had plenty to complain about, including one brief exchange of dialogue, which they insisted had to be removed. It's part of a conversation between the characters of

Robert E. Lee Prewitt (Montgomery Clift) and Alma (Donna Reed):

> Alma: 'Sit down and get comfortable. I'll make you a Martini and see what's to cook for dinner.'
>
> Prewitt: 'Hey, this is like bein' married, ain't it?'
>
> Alma: 'It's better.'

Seems innocuous enough. Not to the MPAA, who pointed out that Prewitt is an Army Private and Alma is a bar-room hostess (synonymous with 'hooker'). For them, that flippant exchange suggested a serious threat to traditional family values by having two unmarried people 'playing house'. The producers refused to cut the line. The censors insisted. Finally they agreed that the line could stay, but the producers were to ensure that the lines were spoken without any 'suggestiveness'. Suggestive or not, Clift was nominated for an Oscar for his performance and Reed won one for hers.

The Follow-up A few years later, Hollywood returned to the twin subjects of author James Jones and Martinis when his novel *Some Came Running* (1959) was brought to the screen. A portrait of a burned-out, disillusioned war veteran (Frank Sinatra) finding it impossible to adjust to life in his small home town, the film includes the words: 'Let me fix you a Martini that's pure magic. It may not make life's problems disappear, but it'll certainly reduce their size.'

BILLY WILDER AND THE MPAA

Throughout the 1950s, the MPAA became increasingly obsessed with the tide of permissiveness that was sweeping the nation. When director Billy Wilder tried to bring George Axlerod's hit stage play *The Seven Year Itch* to the screen in 1955, much of the frankly sexual content had to be toned down. This suggestive exchange between the very married Richard Sherman (Tom Ewell) and the voluptuous object of his wandering eye, The Girl (Marilyn Monroe), was allowed to stand, however:

> Sherman: 'There's gin and vermouth. That's a Martini.'
> The Girl: 'Oh, that sounds cool! I think I'll have a glass of that. A big tall one!'

What Marilyn Monroe could achieve by purring four perfectly innocent words like 'a big tall one' needs no explanation!

Billy Wilder had always courted controversy. His terrifying portrait of alcoholism *The Lost Weekend* (1945) and the ferocious satire *Sunset Boulevard* (1950) had both had to overcome censorship hurdles. Even his classic comedy *Some Like It Hot* (1959) raised eyebrows through its heady mix of speakeasies and transvestites.

Kiss Me, Stupid By the time he came to make the racy comedy *Kiss Me, Stupid* in 1964, Wilder had had enough. It was about an aspiring songwriter (Ray Walston) who hires a floozy (Kim Novak) to

Mid-life crisis: Tom Ewell and an ecstatic Marilyn Monroe in **The Seven Year Itch** *(1955).*

'You're not a drunk if you can lie on the floor without holding on.'

Dean Martin

pose as his wife and seduce a Martini-swilling Las Vegas lounge singer (Dean Martin), thus giving him the ammunition to blackmail the crooner into buying his songs. Knowing that his script would be dismissed out of hand by the MPAA, he simply didn't let them see the screenplay until the film was finished. *Kiss Me, Stupid* was reluctantly passed by the committee – with film already in the can, what else could they do? – although it was later condemned by the Catholic League of Decency.

MARTINIS ON THE BOX

While the MPAA was still disturbed by uncontrolled displays of drinking in the movies right up until the 1960s, it seems to have to escaped their notice that the small screen had become quite accommodating to the Martini.

In 1953, a fantasy sitcom named 'Topper' made its debut on national television. The series was based partly on a 1926 novel by the comic author Thorne Smith, about a hapless banker, Cosmo Topper (Leo G. Carroll), who finds his domestic life turned upside down by the ghosts of a pair of free-spirited socialites who only he can see. The best-selling novel had already served as the basis for a popular trilogy of movies in the late 1930s and early 1940s, but the TV show introduced a new character to the scenario. His name was Neil and he lived for Martinis. Whenever a Martini was placed in front of him, he would just dive straight in and slurp it down. Neil was a St Bernard dog.

A NEW RAT PACK

By the 1950s, Las Vegas had become something of second home to a tightly knit group of entertainers who had consciously modelled themselves on Humphrey Bogart's old drinking circle, the Holmby Hills Rat Pack. At the head of this new, even more disreputable Rat Pack was Frank Sinatra. The other members were Dean Martin (Dino to his friends), singer/dancer Sammy Davis Jr, British actor Peter Lawford and comedian Joey Bishop. Shirley MacLaine, Juliet Prowse and Angie Dickinson sometimes tagged along. Wherever the Pack went, Martinis were sure to follow.

The Rat Pack may not actually have ruled Vegas, but they were certainly five of its most colourful, popular and influential characters. Their unofficial clubhouse was the Copa Room at the Sands Hotel.

With the Rat Packers, it was hard to see where their careers ended and where the party began. Director Lewis Milestone tore his hair out trying to get the quintet to knuckle down for their 1960 ensemble debut *Ocean's Eleven*, a comedy about the attempt to rob five Vegas casinos simultaneously. The boys were a law unto themselves on the set, turning up only when they felt like it and seldom bothering to deliver a performance. The irony is that it didn't matter – *Ocean's Eleven* managed the feat of being both a terrible movie and something of a cult classic. The two official follow-ups – the comedy *Sergeant's 3* (1962) and the musical *Robin and the Seven Hoods* (1964) – also provided a lack of improvement of any sort.

Tight clinch: Dean Martin gets to grips with a Dry Martini and Carol Burnett in Who's Been Sleeping in My Bed? (1963).

As forgettable as those movies may have been, the citizens of Las Vegas had good cause to remember the glory days of the Rat Pack. Those five guys probably did more to promote the town to the general public than the entire Chamber of Commerce. When Frankie and Dino died, the zillions of lights along The Strip were dimmed in honour of the city's two impossible, irrepressible prodigal sons.

DEAN MARTIN – A MAN CALLED MARTINI

When young Italian-American Dino Paul Crocetti set out to make a name for himself in showbusiness he originally called himself Dean Martini, before later settling on the less ethnically specific Dean Martin. Of all the members of the second-generation Rat Pack, Dino was the one who seemed most to live the role. One always seems to picture him with a Martini glass in his hand. His devil-may-care attitude, throwaway style of delivery and apparently permanent state of inebriation suggested a man who cared little for stardom. 'I'd hate to be a teetotaller,' he once said. 'Imagine getting up in the morning and knowing that's as good as you're going to feel all day.' Yet it's also no secret that much of his 'style' was put on. Dino never drank quite as much as his reputation suggested – he was always the first to bed and the earliest to rise – and he conducted his professional career with a ruthlessness that bordered on the pathological.

Consider his treatment of his former partner, Jerry Lewis. As straight man to the rubber-faced comedian, Martin had an impressive 16 consecutive movie hits over the course of ten years.

'If you drink, don't drive. Don't even putt.'

Dean Martin

> 'The only American invention as perfect as a sonnet.'
>
> *H.L. Mencken describing the Martini*

Dry dock: Frank Sinatra and Jill St John enjoy shipboard Martinis in Tony Rome (1967).

Bellini-tini

ice cubes
2 measures vodka
½ measure peach purée
½ measure peach schnapps
4 drops peach bitters
2 peach wedges, to decorate

The combination of peach flavours enhanced by a generous serving of vodka make this a very special drink.

Put the ice cubes into a cocktail shaker, add the vodka, peach purée, peach schnapps and peach bitters and shake well. Strain into a Martini glass and decorate with peach wedges.

Watermelon Martini

ice cubes
½ cup fresh watermelon
2 measures vodka
¼ measure sugar syrup
 (see page 95)
¼ measure Passoa
 (passion fruit liqueur),
 optional
watermelon wedge, to
 decorate

This Martini is the liquid embodiment of exotic summer holidays. Take a sip, close your eyes and you can almost feel the sand underfoot.

Put the ice cubes into a cocktail shaker, add the watermelon, vodka, sugar syrup and Passoa and shake well. Strain into a chilled old-fashioned glass and decorate with a watermelon wedge.

Then, in 1956, he simply dropped Lewis without a second thought. While Lewis continued to profess a fondness for his one-time buddy, Martin only ever referred to Jerry as 'the monkey'.

Dino only ever made a few really good movies – *Rio Bravo* (1959), *Some Came Running* (1959) and *Kiss Me, Stupid* (1964), all of which relied to a greater or lesser extent on his boozy persona – but enjoyed enormous success on television with 'The Dean Martin Show', which had an unbroken run from 1965 to 1974. In later years, Dino became a recluse, and died as he lived – an enigma.

JAMES BOND ARRIVES

By the 1960s, morals in the cinema had loosened up to such an extent that the world was ready for a new novelty. It got one. Its name was Bond ... James Bond. It had taken almost a decade for Ian Fleming's suave secret agent to reach the big screen, although there had been a television version of *Casino Royale* starring Barry Nelson as early as 1954.

The moment the impeccable Sean Connery flashed on screen in *Dr No* in 1962, however, it was obvious that the character was here to stay. There have been 20 Bond movies to date – and that's not counting the spoof *Casino Royale* (1967), the rogue adventure *Never Say Never Again* (1983) and countless spin-offs, rip-offs and homages. Only the giant Japanese monster *Godzilla* has enjoyed a longer run at the world box office.

Overdressed, oversexed and over the top, it's hardly surprising that men wanted to be like Bond and women wanted to meet him. What better way to emulate this screen hero than by adopting his casual insouciance and taste for Vodka Martinis.

BOND'S SPECIAL DRINK

'A Vodka Martini. Shaken, not stirred.' It's one of the great catchphrases in cinema history, invariably spoken by James Bond, alias agent 007, On Her Majesty's Secret Service.

In Ian Fleming's first Bond novel, *Casino Royale*, James explains his drinking ritual to a fellow agent, the beautiful and seductive Vesper Lynd. He outlines a mix of 3 parts gin, 1 part vodka and half a measure of Lillet (a French aperitif, pronounced 'leelay', that blends Bordeaux wine, grape brandy, herbs, spices and fruit), with a twist of lemon. Having fallen heavily for the abundant charms of Lynd, and unaware that she is actually a double agent, Bond names the drink after her – the Vesper.

It was only when Bond reached the movies that this sophisticated recipe was simplified to the famous shaken Vodkatini (see page 36), which has been religiously imbibed on every adventure, with one notorious exception.

In the 1967 film *You Only Live Twice*, while Bond (played by Sean Connery) is in Japan investigating the disappearance of some Russian and American spacecraft, he has a nocturnal meeting with a

'I never have more than one drink before dinner. But I do like that to be large and very strong and very well-made.'

James Bond, in the novel Casino Royale

Of human bondage: Sean Connery as 007, with Joseph Wiseman and Ursula Andress in Dr No (1962).

fellow British agent, Henderson (Charles Gray). As the two sound each other out, Henderson offers Bond his usual Vodka Martini and confirms that he likes the drink 'stirred, not shaken'. Strangely, Bond readily accepts this offer and even qualifies it by saying 'perfect'. Bond fans have discussed the significance of this break from tradition for decades. Is it a bluff on Bond's part? Or a gaffe on Henderson's? Don't forget that the screenplay was written by that master of the unexpected, Roald Dahl – so it may just have been a sly joke at Fleming's expense.

THE MARTINI IN DECLINE

As cinema audiences started to stay in and watch television, the Martini found a new home on the weekly television variety series 'The Dean Martin Show', which ran for a whole decade. Every week, Dino would slide down the fireman's pole into his ersatz bachelor pad and croon his way over to the on-set wet bar, spending much of the rest of the show with a cigarette in one hand, a Martini in the other, and one of his numerous decorative 'dancers' – dubbed the Gold-diggers – draped around his neck.

'... the only green vegetables
I get are Martini olives.'

'Hawkeye', in the TV show 'M*A*S*H'

Strawberry Martini

This cocktail is perfect for early summer drinks in the garden when you can enjoy the wonderful taste of fresh strawberries.

3 fresh strawberries
¼ measure sirop de fraises
(strawberry syrup)
ice cubes
2½ measures vodka
¼ measure dry vermouth
½ strawberry, to decorate

Put the strawberries and sirop de fraises into a mixing glass and muddle together. Transfer to a cocktail shaker, add the ice cubes, vodka and dry vermouth and shake well. Strain into a chilled Martini glass and serve.

Kiwi-tini

½ kiwi fruit, peeled
¼ measure sugar syrup
  (see page 95)
2 measures vodka
½ measure kiwi schnapps
ice cubes
kiwi wheel, to decorate

This drink not only looks cool and elegant but it also tastes exotic.

Put the kiwi fruit into a mixing glass with the sugar syrup and muddle together. Transfer to a cocktail shaker, add the vodka, kiwi schnapps and ice cubes and shake well, then strain into a chilled glass. Strain twice if you want to remove all the kiwi pips, although they look good left in. Decorate with a kiwi wheel and serve.

Similarly, the fantasy sitcom 'Bewitched' made a centrepiece of the lavishly stocked bar in the chaotic home of Samantha and Darrin Stephens (Elizabeth Montgomery and Dick York). If ad executive Darrin wasn't clinching deals with clients over Martinis, he was casually mixing them at home for himself and his long-suffering boss Larry Tate (David White).

Both shows made their debut in the mid-1960s – 'Bewitched' first aired in 1964, with Dino loping along in 1965 – before television developed an acute case of political correctness. Terrified of being accused of promoting unhealthy values, the TV companies sold off the series' wet bars for firewood. Dino also limited his smoking to his dressing room and ditched the Gold-diggers.

M*A*S*H Holds Out The one exception was the long-running 1970s comedy series 'M*A*S*H'. In author Richard Hooker's original novel and Robert Altman's caustic big-screen adaptation in 1970, the irreverent Korean War medics Benjamin Franklin 'Hawkeye' Pierce (played in the movie by Donald Sutherland and in the TV series by Alan Alda) and 'Trapper' John McIntyre (Elliott Gould in the movie and then Wayne Rogers in the TV series) alternated between sewing up the wounded and stitching themselves up with Martinis.

This proclaimed self-indulgence was allowed to continue in the long-running TV series that followed. This is perhaps because the show was set at a point in the past when such behaviour was considered acceptable. Thus 'Hawkeye' was left to carry the torch for the Martini through the 1970s, memorably demanding in one episode: '... a very dry, arid, barren, desiccated, veritable dustbowl of a Martini. I want a Martini that could be declared a disaster area.'

COMEBACK IN THE CINEMA

The Martini had all but vanished from the big screen during the late 1970s and early 1980s, but it managed to put in a few appearances. In 1981, the hardy cocktail played a small but crucial supporting role to the diminutive British comedian Dudley Moore in the hit comedy *Arthur*. In 1984, director Francis Ford Coppola beckoned audiences in to sample the heady delights of the most famous speakeasy of them all, *The Cotton Club* – but the film was a costly and troubled production, and far too few cinema-goers were willing to take up Coppola's invitation.

Resurrection Just at the point when everyone had relegated the Martini to the dustbin of history, it staged the most remarkable comeback. Cocktails were suddenly cool again. The dreadful *Cocktail* (1988) proved to be a unexpected hit for Tom Cruise at the box office. Far more worthy of attention, however, was *The Fabulous Baker Boys* (1989), in which a rumpled Jeff Bridges suddenly made cocktail lounges interesting again. Mind you, having Michelle Pfeiffer roll around atop a grand piano while whispering her way through the song 'Makin' Whoopee' probably helped.

Director Martin Scorsese reacquainted us with the downmarket lounge bars of New York's outer boroughs in the gangster movie *GoodFellas* (1990), before heading over to the glitter palaces of Las Vegas for *Casino* (1995). The Algonquin Round Tablers (see page 20) were brought vividly to life in *Mrs Parker and the Vicious Circle* (1994), with Jennifer Jason Leigh as Dorothy.

A young film-maker called Quentin Tarantino, who had seemingly spent his youth mentally distilling the coolness from world cinema, presented us with *Reservoir Dogs* (1992), whose entire opening restaurant scene is an elaborate pastiche of the 1920s speakeasy.

His subsequent films, *Pulp Fiction* (1994) and *Jackie Brown* (1997), cruised knowledgeably round the lounge bars of Los Angeles. Another young upstart, the talented writer/director Paul Thomas Anderson, demonstrated a casual familiarity with Vegas lounge culture in his offbeat gambling drama *Hard Eight* (1996) as well as the intimate workings of the porn industry in *Boogie Nights* (1997).

Everywhere you looked, the cinema was rediscovering the Martini – along the mean streets of *L.A. Confidential* (1997), during the poker marathons of *Rounders* (1998), and on the well-worn bar stools in *Trees Lounge* (1996). You could even find a gorilla called Amy sipping a consoling Martini in the loopy sci-fi adventure *Congo* (1995). The wheel had turned full circle in 2002 when director Steven Soderbergh remade *Ocean's Eleven*, with George Clooney, Brad Pitt, Matt Damon, Don Cheadle and others affirming their positions as the new Kings of Cool in a slick reworking of the old story.

TV REVIVAL

Television was also ready to rediscover its bad habits. Whereas alcohol had been allowed on the small screen only sparingly since the 1960s, the 1990s managed to introduce a clutch of hip, hit TV shows in which drinking was not depicted as being either dangerous or anti-social. The immaculate, sexy youths of the upmarket soap 'Melrose Place' (1992–1999) chugged cocktails like there was no tomorrow in various bars. Virtually every episode of the legal comedy series 'Ally McBeal' (1997–2002) ended up in the downstairs bar for a round of Martinis and dancing with the music provided by the resident singer and pianist. And the outspoken quartet of free-thinking females in the raunchy sitcom 'Sex and the City' (1998–present) were forever bouncing from the bedroom into the bar-room with Martinis in hand.

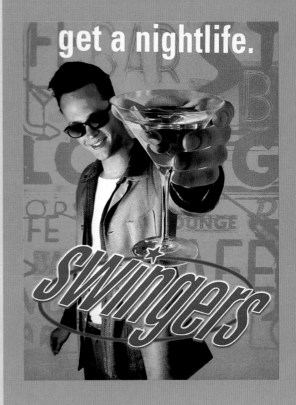

get a nightlife.

Swingers

IN THE SWING

The film that sums up the spirit of the Martini revival was Swingers *(1996). In this collaboration between Jon Favreau and Doug Liman, five Rat Pack wannabes trawl LA in search of love, cocktails and parties. With advice for the modern lounge lizard – from planning a low-budget trip to Vegas to understanding answerphone etiquette – the film demonstrates a wit drier than the driest Martini. The tagline of* Swingers *could yet become the motto of a whole generation: 'Cocktails first. Questions later.'*

73

Rude Cosmopolitan

This tequila-based Martini is deceptively powerful. It has a delicious and subtle combination of fruit flavours.

ice cubes
1½ measures gold tequila
1 measure Cointreau
1 measure cranberry juice
½ measure fresh lime juice
flamed orange twist (see
page 95)

Put the ice cubes into a cocktail shaker, add the gold tequila, Cointreau, cranberry juice and fresh lime juice and shake well. Strain into a chilled Martini glass and decorate with a flamed orange twist.

'The three Martini lunch is the epitome of American efficiency. Where else can you get an earful, a bellyful and a snootful at the same time?'

President Gerald Ford

Wet bar: Dudley Moore relaxes with a Dry Martini in Arthur (1981).

Lemon Martini

ice cubes
1½ measures citron vodka
1 measure fresh lemon juice
¼ measure sugar syrup
  (see page 95)
¼ measure Cointreau
3 drops orange bitters
orange twist

This Martini has a fresh and simple combination of lemon and orange flavours.

Put the ice cubes into a cocktail shaker, add the citron vodka, lemon juice, sugar syrup, Cointreau and orange bitters and shake well. Strain into a chilled Martini glass and add an orange twist.

Shake, rattle and roll: mixing cocktails in the club lounge aboard a Rock Island train.

In the Lounge

Every bar has secrets and every bartender has a story to tell. Here we visit a few of the places that offered the Martini a home and that helped transform it from the makeshift cocktail once presented to a thirsty miner to the crystalline drink sipped by some of the greatest minds, most beautiful faces and most supreme talents of our time.

SAN FRANCISCO

You will never die of thirst in San Francisco – the city has over 2000 bars of all shapes and sizes. Anyone searching for the old Occidental Hotel, however, is in for a disappointment. That exclusive establishment on Montgomery Street, where 'Professor' Jerry Thomas claimed to have mixed the first ever Martini, has long since vanished. It survived the great earthquake and fire that all but levelled the city in 1906, but was eventually torn down to make way for the Russ Building. The 'Prof' himself upped roots and moved to New York to mix drinks at the Metropolitan Hotel in Manhattan.

Redwood Room, Clift Hotel The most venerable of the great San Francisco lounge bars is probably the Redwood Room at the Clift Hotel (495 Geary Street). Despite being located near one of the racier areas of town, the bar offers an oasis of sophistication. Established in 1933, the bar is famous for its magnificent wooden panelling, alleged to have come from a single giant redwood tree. So beloved was the Redwood Room by the San Franciscans that when it was suggested, in 2001, that the bar was to be renovated, they took to the streets in protest. In the end, the facelift was pretty minimal; just a little nip and tuck here and there.

Bix Restaurant You may need some time to locate the secluded Bix Restaurant (56 Gold Street, between Montgomery and Sansome Streets). It's worth the search. Although it's a recent addition to the city's social scene, proprietor Doug 'Bix' Biederbeck still thinks it has played an important role in the history of the Martini: 'I like to think that we helped spark the Martini revival when we opened in 1988. We serve so many that I'm dreading the first case of carpal tunnel syndrome from all the shaking my bartenders do.'

The Bix Restaurant in San Francisco.

The restaurant is a cavernous replica of the famous 1930s New York speakeasy The Cotton Club and features live jazz.

The Purple Onion Nearby, at the base of the Transamerica pyramid, you'll find The Purple Onion (140 Columbus Avenue). Although it is now primarily a rock-music venue, when it opened in the 1950s the basement club was one of the most famous stop-offs on the West Coast cabaret circuit. Lenny Bruce, Phyllis Diller, Mort Sahl, Woody Allen and Barbra Streisand all played there.

Tosca Café For celebrity-spotting in style, try the world-famous Tosca Café (242 Columbus Avenue), in the North Beach District, which offers plush red vinyl booths, an intimate atmosphere and opera on the jukebox. Tosca has proved a magnet for entertainers, politicians and the literati since 1919, and some of its more notable patrons include Bob Dylan, Sam Shepard, Tom Waits and Bono. It's located right by the offices of film-maker Francis Ford Coppola. Tosca Café will also be familiar to film buffs – both *Basic Instinct* (1992) and *Until the End of the World* (1991) have used it as a location. The ladies' room is decorated in homage to screen tough guy Robert Mitchum, while the gents' is a shrine to Marilyn Monroe.

Vesuvio's If the swanky Tosca Café isn't really your style or budget, cross the road and make for Vesuvio's (255 Columbus Avenue) – just look out for the gaudy murals which cover its façade. Inside, the décor is poised somewhere between a dive bar and an Irish pub. Opening in 1948, Vesuvio's became one of the most notorious hangouts for the Beat writers, including Jack Kerouac, Neal Cassady and Allen Ginsberg. Kerouac was such a fixture that the alley that divides the bar from the famous City Lights bookshop next door was renamed Jack Kerouac Alley in his honour.

Spec's A little farther up Jack Kerouac Alley, you'll find Spec's (12 Jack Kerouac Alley), another prime hangout for the Beat poets and their hangers-on. You'll be hard pressed to find a cheaper and more satisfying Martini in the entire city than at this bohemian hideaway.

Hotel Utah There is one historic San Francisco bar that is definitely worth a visit. There has been a saloon at the Hotel Utah (500 4th Street, at Bryant Street) since 1908, when it was part of the notorious Barbary Coast red-light district. In the 1950s it attracted an eclectic crowd, including Marilyn Monroe and hubby Joe DiMaggio, Bing Crosby, and assorted Beats and mobsters. Transformed into a comedy venue in the late 1970s, the Utah has seen the likes of Whoopi Goldberg and Robin Williams cracking wise under its roof.

The 500 Club This bar (500 Guerrero Street, at 17th Street) is a bit of a dive, but the joint earns a mention because of its astonishing façade: a towering neon Martini reaching up to the heavens.

LOS ANGELES

'If you must get in trouble,' warned Hollywood studio executive Harry Cohn to actors William Holden and Glenn Ford, 'do it at the Chateau Marmont.' This famous – or infamous – establishment is as good a place as any to start a crawl through the bars, lounges and clubs of the City of Lost Angels.

Chateau Marmont The Chateau Marmont (8221 Sunset Boulevard) is a bizarre mix of French, Gothic and Art Deco styles.

French Martini

2 measures vodka
½ measure Chambord (see page 94)
1 measure pineapple juice
ice cubes
1 raspberry, to decorate

This creamy blend, sweetened by the pineapple juice, is a real sweet treat.

Put the vodka, Chambord and pineapple juice into a cocktail shaker, add the ice cubes and shake vigorously. Strain into a chilled Martini glass and float a raspberry on top.

Tre Martini

A delicious rum-based Martini with a subtle mingling of flavours.

Empty glass: Bette Davis and Thelma Ritter in All About Eve (1950).

ice cubes
2 measures Havana 3-year-old rum (medium or slightly sweet rum)
¼ measure Chambord (see page 94)
1 measure apple juice
¼ measure sugar syrup
lemon twist

Put the ice cubes into a mixing glass, add the rum, Chambord, apple juice and sugar syrup and stir well. Strain into a chilled glass and add a lemon twist.

Blackberry Martini

2 measures Absolut Kurant
1 measure Crème de Mure
ice cubes
1 blackberry, to decorate

A powerful and very pleasant Martini, with the flavours being provided by Absolute Kurant, a blackcurrant-flavoured vodka and Crème de Mure, a blackberry liqueur.

Put the Absolut Kurant and Crème de Mure into a mixing glass, add the ice cubes and stir well. Strain into a chilled Martini glass and decorate with a blackberry.

Chateau Marmont has attracted celebrity guests since it first opened in 1929. Jean Harlow and Clark Gable met there on the sly, a stoned Jim Morrison once performed a death-defying leap from one of its balconies, and James Dean and Natalie Wood met there to rehearse their lines for *Rebel Without a Cause* (1955). Errol Flynn, Boris Karloff, Paul Newman and Sidney Poitier all checked in, while comic actor John Belushi checked out in 1982 after a drug overdose in Bungalow 3 of the hotel's grounds. The Bar Marmont, with its butterfly ceiling and stuffed peacocks, has also proved a draw with the celebrity crowd, and notable patrons have included Johnny Depp, Winona Ryder and Ellen DeGeneres.

Whiskey Bar, Sunset Marquis Hotel Nearby you'll find another venerable establishment, The Sunset Marquis Hotel (1200 Alta Loma Road). Since first opening in 1963, the hotel and its mellow lounge, the Whiskey Bar, has played host to some of the greatest names in rock music, from the Rolling Stones, Jeff Beck and Neil Young to U2, Courtney Love and Aerosmith. The decor pays homage to guitarist Jimi Hendrix.

The Whisky The Whiskey Bar (see above) should not be confused with The Whisky (8901 Sunset Boulevard), another prime rock-star watering hole. Jim Morrison and The Doors got their break as The Whisky's house band back in 1966. One famous incident occurred during The Beatles' first trip to America in 1964. The band had been invited out for a night on the town by buxom blonde bombshell Jayne Mansfield and they all ended up at The Whisky. After being pestered by a persistent photographer, George Harrison hurled his drink at him ... but he missed and soaked B-movie starlet Mamie Van Doren instead. To think they used to call him the 'Quiet Beatle'!

The Argyle (Sunset Towers) Another local hotel, The Argyle (8358 Sunset Boulevard), was once known as the Sunset Towers. At that time, millionaire playboy Howard Hughes kept a number of suites there for his lady friends, and John Wayne reputedly tethered a cow on the balcony of his room to ensure a ready supply of fresh milk. The Towers has also played host to Charlie Chaplin, Marlene Dietrich and Katharine Hepburn, while Liza Minnelli and Elizabeth Taylor numbered among the members of its exclusive private club. Scenes from the movie *The Player* were shot there in 1992.

Rainbow Bar and Grill Farther along Sunset Boulevard, you'll find the Rainbow Bar and Grill (9015 Sunset Boulevard). The establishment is built on the site of the old Villa Nova restaurant, a romantic retreat where Marilyn Monroe and Joe DiMaggio enjoyed their first date, and where film director Vincente Minnelli proposed to Judy Garland. It still attracts a starry crowd, including Jack Nicholson, Sylvester Stallone, Nicolas Cage and Robin Williams.

Sunset Trocadero In Old Hollywood, three clubs dominated Sunset Boulevard: The Mocambo, Ciro's and The Trocadero. Lucille Ball and Desi Arnaz, Dean Martin, Jerry Lewis, Eartha Kitt and Josephine Baker were all regulars at Ciro's, Frank Sinatra had an altercation with the paparazzi on its doorstep, and Mae West once judged a bodybuilding competition there. Meanwhile, Edith Piaf and Lena Horne famously performed at The Mocambo. Although all three clubs are now little more than distant memories, a revamped Sunset Trocadero (8280 West Sunset Boulevard) has since opened across the road. This modern lounge has mimicked the Art Deco ambience of the original nightspot, and is a popular haunt for the kings of New Hollywood, including Mark Wahlberg and Leonardo DiCaprio.

The Viper Room One other nearby symbol of New Hollywood has achieved fame for entirely different reasons. The Viper Room (8852 Sunset Boulevard) has been immortalized as the site on which the promising young actor River Phoenix had his career cut short by a fatal seizure in 1993.

Musso & Frank's Over on Hollywood Boulevard, Musso & Frank's (6667 Hollywood Boulevard) boasts the double claim of being Tinseltown's first ever restaurant as well as its longest running. Opened in 1919 by John Musso and Frank Toulet, it has proved a refuge for both the literati and the glitterati. F. Scott Fitzgerald, William Faulkner and Dashiell Hammett were all regulars. It is even reputed that Raymond Chandler finished writing *The Big Sleep* (1939) on the premises. It's one restaurant that never seems to go out of style. In the old days, the clientele included silent star Tom Mix, Charlie Chaplin, Paulette Goddard and Humphrey Bogart. These days, you're likely to find Ben Kingsley and Al Pacino rubbing shoulders with Sean Penn, Brad Pitt and film director David Lynch.

Windows Lounge, Four Seasons Hotel In nearby Beverly Hills is the Four Seasons Hotel (300 South Doheny Drive), whose Windows Lounge is one of the more select watering holes in the city and serves its Martinis in mini-pitchers. At Frank Sinatra's 80th birthday party in 1996, he gathered buddies Tony Bennett, Steve Lawrence, Eydie Gorme, Robert Wagner and Jill St John around the piano for an impromptu singalong.

Palomar Ballroom The Palomar Ballroom, which stood at Vermont Avenue and Second Street until it was razed by fire in 1939, became 'Jitterbug Central' after bandleader Benny Goodman sparked the craze for swing music there in 1935. Some who made their names at the Palomar and its dance-hall rival Bourston's went on to lasting fame. These included Dean Collins and Jewel McGowan, who were immortalized in movies such as *Hellzapoppin'* (1941) and *The Horn Blows at Midnight* (1945).

Venice Beach In the early part of the century, the district of Venice Beach established itself as one of the great leisure destinations for Los Angelinos, with its coastline, amusement parks and arcades. The fun continued in the 1920s, when a number of speakeasies sprang up all along Windward Avenue, with bootleg booze being smuggled through secret tunnels from the beach into the various shady establishments.

The Georgian Hotel Likewise, out in Santa Monica, The Georgian Hotel (1415 Ocean Avenue) once housed one of the city's most celebrated speakeasies. The guests ranged from the famous – Clark Gable and Carole Lombard were regulars – to the infamous, including the disgraced comedian Roscoe 'Fatty' Arbuckle and glamorous gangster Benjamin 'Bugsy' Siegel.

Gambler's Row Just 5km (3 miles) off the coast of Santa Monica lies the site of one of the great Prohibition loopholes called 'Gambler's Row'. It was a bootlegger called Tony Cornero and a mobster named Johnny Roselli who decided to take advantage of the fact that America's drinking and gambling laws did not apply to vessels at sea. They bought and refurbished a fleet of fishing boats and barges, anchored them a suitable distance from the coast and ferried partygoers to and fro aboard water taxis. One of the most famous of the vessels on Gambler's Row was the SS *Rex*.

Pale Original

ice cubes
2 measures gold tequila
½ measure ginger syrup
½ measure fresh lime juice
1 measure guava juice
lime wedges, to decorate

Another tequila-based Martini, this is a sweet and sour cocktail with a long ginger finish.

Put the ice cubes, gold tequila, ginger syrup, lime juice and guava juice into a cocktail shaker and shake well. Strain into a chilled glass and serve.

Off the shoulder: Jack Lemmon cosies up to Virna Lisi in How to Murder Your Wife (1965).

Vanilla Martini

1 vanilla pod
¼ measure vanilla syrup
2½ measures vanilla vodka
(see page 95)
¼ measure dry vermouth
ice cubes

This is a very popular Martini, with a soft, mellow flavour from the fresh vanilla.

Put the vanilla pod and vanilla syrup in a mixing glass and muddle together.
Add the vanilla vodka, dry vermouth and ice cubes and shake well. Strain into a
chilled Martini glass and serve,

After the repeal of Prohibition, Tony Cornero switched his attention to Vegas, where he opened the SS *Rex* Club as a tribute to his lucrative maritime venture. Cornero had grand plans to build a vast casino hotel complex in Vegas, but suffered a fatal heart attack while at the gaming tables and never realized his dream.

Lola's One of the most venerated of LA's lounge bars, Lola's (945 North Fairfax Avenue, West Hollywood) offers over 40 different varieties of Martini, including their own house speciality: the Green Apple Martini, which comes garnished with a slice of Granny Smith.

LAS VEGAS

Anyone travelling to Vegas to sample a little of the cool ambience of the 1950s and 1960s will be disappointed. Most of the original landmarks have gone in the property developers' quest to erect ever larger and more glitzy pleasure domes to service the world's gamblers. In 1996, a tiny slice of American popular history came to an end when the original Sands Hotel was torn down to make way for the new Venetian casino resort. The Copa Room, notorious stomping-ground of the Rat Pack, was no more. Ironically, the first of the great casino hotels – El Rancho – was one of the very last to go in 2000, although by then it had fallen into disrepair.

Drinking Lounges With most visitors preferring to imbibe in the casinos themselves – where the drinks are free as long as you are gambling – more and more Las Vegas lounges have had to adopt elaborate and gaudy gimmicks in order to pull in the punters.

In the Horse-Around-Bar (Circus Circus, 2880 Las Vegas Boulevard South), drinkers are enclosed within a giant revolving carousel. In the Hookah Lounge (Tiffany Square, 4147 South Maryland Parkway), guests can alternate sips of their Martinis with puffs from the ornate Turkish pipes. The Shadow Bar (Caesar's Palace, 3750 Las Vegas Boulevard South) has body-stockinged dancers gyrating in silhouette behind screens. Even the highly regarded and relatively restrained cocktail bar at Bellagio (3600 Las Vegas Boulevard South) makes a feature of the dancing fountains and replica Eiffel Tower which can be glimpsed through its windows.

You're better advised to go over to the Polo Lounge (Polo Towers, 3745 Las Vegas Boulevard South), where you can gawk at the fountains in a far more relaxing atmosphere. Other models of restraint can be found at the Algiers Cocktail Lounge (2845 Las Vegas Boulevard) and the Allegro Lounge (3600 Las Vegas Boulevard South), the latter of which also features regular sets by Filipino jazz phenomenon Boy Katindig and his band.

NEW YORK

Until 11 September 2001, any guide to the lounge bars of New York would have begun with Windows on the World, the restaurant on the top of the twin towers of the World Trade Center. Sipping a Martini while gazing down at the lights of Manhattan 400m (a quarter of a mile) beneath you was not an experience to be easily forgotten. So it is with great sadness that we have to begin our trip uptown instead.

Algonquin Hotel Established in 1902, the Algonquin (59 West 44th Street) was already considered one of the most venerable hotels in the city by 1919, so the arrival of the Round Tablers for their regular lunch dates (see page 20) only served to increase its fame. The hotel's Blue Bar is an oasis of civilization amid the often manic bustle of midtown Manhattan. While you lounge in the tasteful opulence of its decor, you can ruminate on the many famous names

Gone but not forgotten: the former El Rancho, the first of the great Vegas casino resorts, as it looked in 1958.

who have swept through its doors: writers George Bernard Shaw, John Steinbeck, Simone de Beauvoir, Maya Angelou, W.B. Yeats, William Faulkner and Booth Tarkington.

Tony Soma's and the 21 Club

In the evening the Round Tablers would invariably while away the hours at one of the city's speakeasies, this generally meant either Tony Soma's or the 21 Club (21 West 52nd Street), which was operated by Jack Kriendler and Charlie Burns, two of the city's famous 'hosts'.

Kriendler and Burns opened their first speakeasy, the Red Head in Greenwich Village, in 1922. When that was closed by the police,

the pair were undeterred and simply opened up another one, the Fronton, in Washington Place. This was followed by Jack and Charlie's Puncheon Bowl on West 49th Street, at which point the Algonquin crowd moved in and became regulars. The 21 Club opened in 1929, boasting a secret wine cellar and a complex lever-and-pulley system which would dump all the bottles behind the bar into the sewer system at the first hint of a police raid. Its clientele included actors, musicians, writers, sportsmen and politicians.

After the repeal of Prohibition, the 21 Club went legit and is now one of the city's most exclusive restaurants, instantly recognizable by the kitschy statues of racing jockeys that line the stairway up to its

The bar in the Rainbow Room in the Rockefeller Center.

door. It has been claimed that every US President since Franklin D. Roosevelt has eaten in the restaurant. In 1945, Robert Benchley's memorial service was held there after his death from a cerebral haemorrhage, and there is a plaque on the wall by his favourite table which says 'Robert Benchley – His Corner'. The establishment is also familiar to film buffs, having been used as a location in *All About Eve* (1950), *The Sweet Smell of Success* (1957), *Wall Street* (1987), *Manhattan Murder Mystery* (1993) and *One Fine Day* (1996).

The Rainbow Room Tony Soma's speakeasy was on West 49th Street, just across the road from Jack and Charlie's Puncheon Bowl. There is a certain irony in the fact that these two illicit establishments were knocked down in 1931 to make way for what is now one of the most famous – and legitimate – lounge bars in New York: the Rainbow Room. You can find the Rainbow Room on the 65th floor of the Rockefeller Center (30 Rockefeller Plaza). This towering 'city in the city' was built by philanthropist John D. Rockefeller as a gift to New Yorkers during the Great Depression and the view from the bar is among the most impressive in the city. In 1998, the Cipriani family from Italy, who had achieved worldwide fame with Harry's Bar in Venice, were invited to take over the running of the gastronomic facilities of the Rainbow Room. Most of the time it is only available for private functions. However, it is open to the public for cocktails on selected Fridays and Saturdays, so be sure to call in advance the next time you're planning to be in the city and see whether they can squeeze you in for a Martini or two.

Flute Another historic midtown bar that is well worth a visit is Flute (205 West 54th Street), which was formerly the speakeasy Club Intime run by the legendary hostess 'Texas' Guinan (see page 16). Although, as its name suggests, the bar specializes in champagne, some cocktails are also on the menu. It's a cosy cellar bar perfect for romantic liaisons. In case you were wondering, the trapdoor in the floor is where they used to dump the booze during police raids.

The Cotton Club and Small's Paradise Travel uptown into Harlem and, at 133rd Street, you'll find the former location of two of the most famous speakeasies in the city's history: The Cotton Club and Small's Paradise.

The Cotton Club opened its doors in 1923 after mobster Owney Madden bought the defunct Club De Lux from heavyweight boxer Jack Johnson, transforming the semicircular room into a faux jungle with the help of decorative palm trees. In the politically incorrect climate of the 1920s, Madden's establishment had a strict 'whites only' door policy and became a regular haunt for Fanny Brice, Irving

Berlin, Cole Porter, Bing Crosby and Jimmy Durante, as well as assorted local gangsters and politicians. In marked contrast to the audience, the performers at the Cotton Club were almost entirely black and the impressive roster of stars who made their names at the venue include Duke Ellington, Dorothy Dandridge, Cab Calloway, Lena Horne, Ethel Waters and Bill 'Bojangles' Robinson. The stars of the show were never allowed to mix with the guests and instead had to nip next door to 646 Lenox for booze and marijuana.

The nearby speakeasy Ed Small's Paradise was established in 1926 and offered a far more liberal door policy, welcoming both blacks and whites into the audience. It went on to become the longest-running and most authentic of all the Harlem nightclubs. One charming quirk of the Paradise was that all of the waiters were dancers and prided themselves that they could do the Charleston while burdened with trays of drinks and food. It was a gimmick that

A doorman stands outside the famous Cotton Club in Harlem, New York.

attracted visitors from around the country. The speakeasy continued to do a roaring trade throughout Prohibition, even after a police station was built right across the road in 1932. The Paradise closed its doors for good in 1964.

Café Society In 1938, even greater advances in racial integration were being made back down in Greenwich Village. New Jersey shoe-store owner Barney Josephson decided to sell his business in order to go into partnership with jazz critic John Hammond and bandleader Benny Goodman, the man who had reputedly started the swing craze in Los Angeles three years earlier. Their concept was to open a jazz and comedy venue which would accept whites and blacks alike. It was called Café Society and it was officially the first racially integrated nightclub in America.

Café Society proved an instant success, particularly with the bohemian, politically left-of-centre denizens of the Village. Among the legendary acts who first made their names at Café Society was Blues singer Billie Holiday, who unveiled 'Strange Fruit' there to a wildly enthusiastic crowd, and the comedians Zero Mostel and Jack Gilford. Sadly, it was the club's liberal credo that proved its downfall. At the height of the 'red scare' during the McCarthy witch-hunts of the 1950s, the club's staff and clientele came under investigation for supposed communist sympathies and it was hounded out of business.

Angel's Share When you have had your fill of history, there is one modern cocktail bar that will allow you to just sit quietly and savour your Martini. Locating the East Village bar in question, Angel's Share, isn't easy. This is partly because it is discreetly signposted and, depending on who's giving the directions, is either described as

Chocolate Mint Martini

ice cubes
2 measures vodka
½ measure crème de menthe
1 measure white crème de cacao
½ measure dry vermouth
saucer sprinkled with powdered drinking chocolate

This chocolate and peppermint-flavoured vodka Martini is like a liquid after-dinner mint; it has a very powerful kick.

Put the ice cubes, vodka, crème de menthe, crème de cacao and dry vermouth into mixing glass and stir well. Moisten the rim of a chilled Martini glass with sugar syrup and invert the glass into the powdered chocolate to coat the rim. Pour in the blended drink.

`... civilization in a glass

Noël Coward describing
the Martini

Martini Royale

2½ measures frozen vodka
¼ measure crème de
** Cassis**
Champagne, to top up
lemon twist

If you ever need an excuse to celebrate, just serve this Martini. This cocktail is built in the glass so it is essential that the vodka is kept in the freezer.

Pour the vodka into a chilled martini glass then stir in the Cassis. Top up with Champagne then add a lemon twist.

being at 6 Astor Place or at 8 Stuyvesant Street. You then have to duck indoors, go through to the back and negotiate your way upstairs until you find the right door.

The sleek décor and subdued lighting are genuinely inviting and the Martinis, expertly mixed by the hip Asian staff, are out of this world. There are strict house rules which must be observed, however: no standing, no shouting or singing, no parties of more than four people. Spend your time at Angel's Share in contemplation, in intimate conversation, or simply watching the funky East Villagers going about their business.

AROUND THE WORLD

While it is true that the best Martinis in the world are mixed in the USA, you can probably find yourself a decent Martini anywhere in the world if you are prepared to search long and hard enough. And a handful of international bars not only serve their Martinis perfectly mixed and chilled but have also somehow added to the mystique of this world-class beverage.

London Try the American Bar at the luxurious Savoy Hotel on The Strand. Some lucky people were there on the evening that

The American Bar at the Savoy Hotel in London.

Sammy Davis Jr performed a soft-shoe shuffle atop the bar's grand piano while Frank Sinatra stroked the ivories and sang!

Rome During the production boom at the Cinecitta film studio during the 1950s and 1960s, Marcello Mastroianni, Anita Ekberg, Ava Gardner and Tyrone Power all cooled off at the Café Doney along the Via Vittorio Veneto. Marlon Brando, ever the rebel, preferred the Café de Paris just across the road.

Venice When on the Adriatic, you can enjoy a Martini at Harry's Bar on the St Mark's Bay waterfront – but, be warned, they frown upon the use of an olive as garnish. Since Guiseppe Cipriani opened its doors in 1931, the bar has played host to Orson Welles, Henry Fonda, Maria Callas, Truman Capote, Ernest Hemingway (of course) and even the Aga Khan. More recent converts have been Woody Allen, Nicole Kidman and Helen Hunt.

Harry's Bar in Venice, Italy.

Paris Ernest Hemingway has made his presence felt in Paris on more than one occasion. His famous request for 73 Martinis at the Ritz Hotel (15 Place Vendome), on behalf of a squad of American GI's helping to liberate Paris during World WarTwo, led to them name the bar after him. One of the most famous recent additions to the city's nightlife is named in honour of the world-famous fashion photographer Man Ray (34 Rue Marbeuf). This Eastern-themed bar and restaurant attracts a crowd as starry as its co-owners: Johnny Depp, Sean Penn and Mick Hucknell.

Buenos Aires The Argentine capital of Buenos Aires resounds to the sound of the tango, nowhere more so than at the Café Tortoni (829 Avenida de Mayo). Jorge Luis Borges, Ernesto Sabato, Honoré de Balzac, Edouard Manet, Luigi Pirandello, Federico Garcia Lorca and even Hillary Rodham Clinton have all ruminated in its comfortingly dark corners. When the weight of the world becomes unbearable, there are live jazz and tango to be found in the basement bar, La Bodega.

Singapore In the colonial splendour of the garden at Raffles Hotel, it might seem churlish not to order a Singapore Sling, but it's unlikely that W. Somerset Maugham would have forgone a Martini – stirred, of course – as he put pen to paper in that very spot. Don't forget to sample the Writer's Bar, indoors, where the likes of Joseph Conrad, Rudyard Kipling, Gunter Grass, Noël Coward and Herman Hesse have all pursued their muse.

Glossary

CHAMBORD Royale Chambord Liqueur is a black raspberry flavoured liqueur made in France. Black raspberries are infused with a fine cognac that has been aged for at least four years in oak barrels. After this basic infusion, red raspberry, currants and blackberry extracts are added, along with spices and several other herbs, orange and lemon after that. Acacia honey is also added before the entire mixture is aged in barrels.

This black raspberry liqueur pours a deep purple colour and the scent is pure sweet berry. While this does have a texture slightly thicker than water, it is not syrupy in the least. The bottle is clear glass, but round in shape. There is gold plastic around the outside of the bottle with the Chambord name inserted. The cap is in the shape of a gold crown.

CHOCOLATE SYRUP Whisk 300 g (12 oz) of cocoa powder, 50 ml (2 fl oz) of vanilla syrup and 50 ml (2 fl oz) of hazlenut syrup with 100 ml (3½ fl oz) of boiling water. It will be quite thin to start with, but it will thicken to a glossy syrup as it cools.

FLAMED ORANGE TWIST Slice a disc of orange rind off the side of an orange. Hold a lit match against the rind side of the disc and squeeze the disc between your thumb and forefinger so that it bends. The oils released from the rind will ignite releasing a flame and a strong aroma. Drop the disc into the drink to impart the orange aroma to the cocktail. Please note that this should always be carried out with great care as the it can sometimes produces a surprisingly large flame.

KRUPNIK VODKA This is a Polish honey liqueur. It is prepared from bee honey and blended with various spices and aromatic herbs and is made according to Polish recipes that are hundreds of years old.

LILLET A French fortified wine that is mixed with gin, vodka and lemon to create the Martini that James Bond favoured in *Casino Royale*. A blend of wines selected from the most prestigious wine growing area in the world (Bordeaux) are mixed with fruit liqueurs to make this special drink. Always serve chilled.

SLOE GIN Sloes are small sour wild plums, the fruit of the blackthorn. To make sloe gin you need 1.2 litres (2 pints) gin and 175–250 g (6–8 oz) sugar to each 500 g (1 lb) sloes. Wash the sloes and prick them 5–6 times with a needle and put them into a sterilized container, add the gin, sugar and ¼ teaspoon almond essence and stir well. Cover the container tightly and set it aside for at least 3 months, shaking it once a week. Siphon into bottles and cork securely. Sloe gin made from fruit picked in September or October should be ready to drink by Christmas, although keeping it longer is all to the good.

STOLICHNAYA RAZBERI This is an authentic, natural raspberry-flavoured vodka originating from Russia. Starting with the finest spirits distilled from wheat and clear glacial water, it is then married with the aromatic essence of fresh raspberries to achieve its distinctive taste.

SUGAR SYRUP Again, sugar syrup (Syrup de Gomme) can be bought from good liquor stores but it is relatively easy to make your own. Mix 2 parts of caster sugar with 1 part of boiling water to your desired quantity. Stir well so that the sugar dissolves. It will thicken to a syrup as it cools.

TOUSSAINT Liqueur de café Toussaint is named after the architect of Haiti's independence, General Toussaint L'Ouverture, also known as Napoléon Noir. Toussaint was born in 1743 on the French Carribean island of St Dominique, the Western part of which became the independent republic of Haiti in 1804. It is a rich, coffee-flavoured liqueur and can be replaced with Kahlua if you cannot find Toussaint in your local liquor store.

VANILLA VODKA You can buy Vanilla Vodka from most good liquor stores, but for an extra fresh taste try making your own. Place 2–3 whole vanilla pods in a full bottle of vodka of your choice. Leave to infuse for a week or two and then add to cocktails such as the Vanilla Martini on page 85.

ZUBROWKA VODKA A genuine Polish vodka made which is a result of a tradition going back to the 14th century. Zubrowka is a unique product flavoured with bison grass. It owes its name to an aromatic grass grown wild in the eastern part of Poland, where bison live in their natural habitat. In every bottle a single blade is placed confirming the Polish origin and bottling of the vodka. It is at its best served straight from the freezer.

Index

Algonquin Hotel 20
Anderson, Sherwood 21
Aviation 22

bars 77–8, 82–3, 86–9, 92–3
Bellini-tini 66
Blackberry Martini 81
Bogart, Humphrey 60–1, 64
Bond, James 34, 68–9
bootleg gin 16–17
Buenos Aires 93
Buñuel, Luis 57–8

Chambord 94
Chocolate Mint Martini 90
chocolate syrup 94
Chocotini 54
Clift, Montgomery 62
cocktail lounges 25–6, 31
cocktail shakers 40
Connery, Sean 34, 68
Cosmopolitan 32

Davis, Bette 60, 61, 62
Decatini 55

Dry Martini 9, 10
Fields, W.C. 53, 54, 56
films 50–3, 56–65, 68–9,
    70–1
Fleming, Ian 31, 34, 68
French Martini 79

Gable, Clark 60
gangsters 16, 30, 56–7
garnishes 41, 44–5
The Gibson 45
Gimlet 18
gin 7, 39
glasses 40, 41
Grant, Cary 58, 60
Guinan, 'Texas' 16

ice 45

Kiwi-tini 71
Krupnik vodka 94

Las Vegas 26–7, 30, 31,
    64–5, 86
Lemon Martini 75

Lewis, Jerry 65, 68
Lillet 94
London 92–3
Los Angeles 78, 82–3, 86

Maraschino 40
Martin, Dean 31, 49, 64, 65,
    68, 69
Martinez 8
Martini Royale 91
'M*A*S*H' 72
Monroe, Marilyn 63
music 48–9
myths 47–8

Nash, Ogden 27
New York 86–9
Nixon, Richard 35

olives 41, 44
Opal Martini 29
orange bitters 40
orange twist, flamed 94

Pale Original 84

Paris 93
Polish Martini 37
Prohibition 12–17, 24–5, 30
Raft, George 53, 56–7
Rat Pack 31, 64–5
Rome 93
Roosevelt, F.D. 24, 27
Rude Cosmopolitan 74

Sake-tini 33
San Francisco 77–8
shaking Martinis 47
Sinatra, Frank 31, 49, 62, 64,
    65, 66
Singapore 93
sloe gin 94
Smoky 28
speakeasies 14–16, 25
stirring Martinis 46–7
Stolichnaya Razberi 94
Strawberry Martini 70
sugar syrup 95

television 64, 69, 72, 73
The Thin Man 58–9

Thomas, 'Professor' Jerry 8
Toussaint 95
Tre Martini 80
Turner, Lana 57
Vanilla Martini 85
Vanilla Vodka 95
Venice 93
vermouth 7, 39
Vesper 32
Vochacino 42
vodka 31, 34
Vodkatini 36, 68–9

Watermelon Martini 67
West, Mae 53, 56, 60
White Elephant 42
White Lady 19
Wilder, Billy 62–4
World War Two 27, 30

Zoom 54
Zubrowka vodka 95

acknowledgments

British Film Institute Stills, Posters & Designs 51
Corbis UK Ltd 8, 10, 13, 14, 16, 17 right, 20, 21, 24, 25, 26, 27, 28, 31, 34, 35, 48, 87, 89 /Bob Krist 88 /Kevin Fleming 77 /David Lees 93
Getty Images 22, 47, 49, 66, 76
Octopus Publishing Group Ltd. /Stephen Conroy 1, 2, 5, 6, 11, 18, 19, 23, 29, 32, 33 left, 33 right, 37 left, 37 right, 38, 41, 43, 44, 45, 55, 67, 70 bottom, 71, 74, 79, 81, 84 left, 85, 90, 91 left, 91 right, 95 /Bill Reavell 40
Kobal Collection 3, 9, 54, 60, 70 top, 80
The Moviestore Collection 58
Rex Features/Timepix 42
The Ronald Grant Archive 15, 36, 50, 52, 57, 59, 61, 62, 63, 65, 69, 73, 75, 84 right
Savoy Group Archives 92
Topham Picturepoint 17 left

The author would like to thank: Jane Birch, Sarah Ford, Sheena Harvey, Abi Rowsell, Geoff Fennell.
   Patrick Humphries and Colin Davis graciously filled gaps in my musical knowledge.
   Along with all the books mentioned and quoted in the text, Frank Miller's *Censored Hollywood: Sex, Sin & Violence on Screen* helped in my understanding of Hollywood's censorship battles.

Photographer: Stephen Conroy
Cocktails written and styled by Allan Gage at Grand Central, Great Eastern Road, London
Stylist: Amy Hearn